M000101290

CELEBRATE YOUR MISTAKES

CELEBRATE YOUR MISTAKES

and 77 Other Risk-Taking, Out-of-the-Box Ideas from Our Best Companies

JOHN W. HOLT, JR.

JON STAMELL

MELISSA FIELD

IRWIN
Professional Publishing®
Chicago • London • Singapore

© John W. Holt, Jr., Jon Stamell, and Melissa Field, 1996

All rights reserved. No part of this publication may be
reproduced, stored in a retrieval system, or transmitted,
in any form or by any means, electronic, mechanical,
photocopying, recording, or otherwise, without the prior
written permission of the publisher.

This publication is designed to provide accurate and
authoritative information in regard to the subject matter
covered. It is sold with the understanding that neither the
author nor the publisher is engaged in rendering legal, accounting,
or other professional service. If legal advice or other expert
assistance is required, the services of a competent professional
person should be sought.

*From a Declaration of Principles jointly adopted by a Committee
of the American Bar Association and a Committee of Publishers.*

Times Mirror
Higher Education Group

Library of Congress Catatoging-in-Publication Data

Holt, John W.
    Celebrate your mistakes : and 77 other risk-taking, out-of-the-box
ideas from our best companies / John W. Holt, Jr., Jon Stamell,
Melissa Field.
        p.   cm.
    Includes index.
    ISBN 0-7863-0486-3
    1. Success in business. 2. Management. 3. Risk-taking
(Psychology) 4. Executives–United States–Attitudes. I. Stamell,
Jon. II. Field, Melissa. III. Title.
HF5386.H673 1996
658.4'09—dc20   96–6307

Printed in the United States of America
1 2 3 4 5 6 7 8 9 0 BP 3 2 1 0 9 8 7 6

Acknowledgments

About two years ago, after we presented our company to a consultant named Yustin Wallrapp, he commented, "You seem to do things differently. You ought to write a book." After several thousand hours of concept meetings, outlines, synopses, interviews, and draft after draft after draft, our enthusiasm for Wallrapp's idea has come to fruition. Deciding whether *Celebrate Your Mistakes,* which incidentally was written under the working title of *Pollyannas in the Boardroom,* is an accurate reflection of our doing things differently is ultimately up to you. As authors, we can't help but be too close to our work to offer an objective opinion. Even so, we believe you'll find some ideas in the next 200-odd pages that you never thought of before. If as a result of our writing we can make you think a little differently, laugh at yourself, or try something new, we will have succeeded.

We have Yustin to thank for the initial idea, but there are many others whom we must thank and without whom we could not have gotten this far. First and foremost, Kendra Bonnett, our stalwart writer who synthesized our ideas and reworked many drafts to make us happy with the end result, deserves our gratitude and a purple heart. Jenna Hartel is our company's Knowledge Navigator. Her research skills, fact checking, and willingness to nudge us all along made the job easier and kept us on task. Jenna also became the conscience of the project, ensuring that we maintained high standards throughout.

We've always wondered why George Hughes, the talented illustrator and third partner of our marketing communications firm, Holt, Hughes & Stamell (HHS), hangs around with people like us. With his talent, George could have had a much easier life than we can offer. This book, ostensibly about business but really about life, is very much enriched by George's irreverent illustrations. Mark Nestor, an art director with HHS who seems to work all night every night, deserves our thanks for his ideas and for the design that resulted in Palo Amtman's cover and frontispiece illustrations.

The Holt, Hughes & Stamell staff of advertising account executives, public relations practitioners, copywriters, art directors, and production managers listened to our ideas, helped flesh out the chapters, and gave us positive and negative feedback. Some may have thought this book would never come about, but they never cut back on their participation and enthusiasm. Many of our clients, too, contributed their ideas and took an interest in the project and our thinking. We owe them all our gratitude.

The 12 subjects of our interviews—author and cooking teacher Julia Child, investment guru Michael Stolper, former president of the 1994 Winter Olympics Gerhard Heiberg, mutual fund manager Richard Aster, cable television visionary Rory Strunk, education and entertainment entrepreneur Marshall Smith, computer electronics mover and shakers. S. Robert Levine, organizational consultant Linda Whiteside, marketing consultant Richard Roth, Maine governor Angus King, supermarket executive Hugh Farrington, and media developer Jim Shaffer—all gave us more than their interview responses. As they questioned us about the project and our thought processes, they helped us crystallize our ideas.

Consultant Mark Stevens helped us through the early stages and gave us the confidence to say, "I believe, I believe." And publisher Jeffrey Krames led us through the byzantine world of publishing with sure-handed guidance. We learned from Jeff that no book is the sole work of one or two people who have all the answers. We owe thanks to the many people who have been involved and believed in our project.

Finally, we'd like to thank you for deciding to read *Celebrate Your Mistakes* and want to take this opportunity to ask a favor of you as well. Give us your comments and feedback. Tell us what worked for you and what you'll take with you. Tell us about one of your mistakes and what you learned to celebrate. That way we'll all continue learning together. You can reach any of us at the Internet addresses below. Thank you.

John W. Holt, Jr., jholtjr@hhs.com
Jon Stamell, jonstamell@hhs.com
Melissa Field, melissafield@hhs.com

Contents

Preface

It's been said that doctors bury their mistakes, lawyers hang theirs, and journalists put theirs on the front page. To entrepreneurs, company executives, and employees on all menus of the corporate food chain, we say: Celebrate your mistakes.

This is an idea that's going to take some getting used to. Since childhood, we've all practiced and perfected a game of hide-and-seek in which we learned to hide a myriad of goofs and blunders. In keeping with our stature we started small, hiding as best we could the broken glass or the lost mitten from any adult who happened to be in charge. School proved to be a training ground for perfecting our habits. Each mistake that resulted in a bad grade or detention was a reminder of our failings and, as such, best ignored, forgotten, and above all hidden not only from our parents but also from ourselves. By the time we entered the workforce, we had the skill of denying our mistakes down to an exact science. And so it went.

Today, few of us are spared the myopia that prevents us from seeing anything but success. "Top of the world, Ma," actor Jimmy Cagney shouted in the movie *White Heat,* just seconds before he was blown to smithereens. And believe it or not, there is a lesson here. Rather than focusing only on our successes—both real and imagined—we should promote our mistakes and learn from them. These observations may just save our businesses from disaster.

To remain open to your mistakes, you have to be more perceptive, more open to trying new ideas, more willing to change, and less convinced of your infallibility. In this book we focus on the growing phenomenon in which large companies and small—blinded by years of success amid the harsh realities of an evolving marketplace—come to feel invincible. What they actually are feeling—although they seldom realize it at the time—is the isolation, arrogance and complacency that comes from celebrating too much success while quietly sweeping the mistakes under the rug.

The inspiration for *Celebrate Your Mistakes* came from our own experiences. And to show we are serious, we will kick off this book with each of us celebrating a personal mistake. As you read about our missteps and mishaps, note that mistakes do not have to be earth-shattering to teach us important lessons about life and business. The point in each case is that no matter how bad we felt at the time, we did not bury the experience deep in our unconscious minds. Rather we learned and went on.

John W. Holt, Jr.

After more than 25 years in marketing, my mistakes come in a variety of shapes and sizes. For example, when I started working as the director of advertising at Shop 'n Save supermarkets, one of my first responsibilities was to design a new in-store sign package to be used in 100 supermarkets. We spent considerable time and money on this new design. We considered everything (we thought)—color, design, message. We even took measurements from the local-area stores to ensure we designed the proper sizes.

However, upon receipt of the sign kits, at least 25 percent of the managers called to say their stores were too small and their ceilings too low to accommodate the new signs. To assume all stores were like our local ones was an expensive mistake.

Regardless of the cost to the company, a mistake of this size might easily have joined the multitude of little errors we ignore each day. If nothing else, celebrating all your mistakes—even the little ones—will help you keep your ego and your business on a balanced course.

Today, as director of strategic planning at Holt, Hughes & Stamell (HHS), I have helped develop strategic communications plans for major U.S. companies such as BF Goodrich, Connecticut Mutual Life Insurance, Glen Ellen wines, Hamilton Beach appliances, Marshall's, Hannaford Bros. Co., and LL Bean. I believe in the ultimate wisdom of the saying, "Measure twice and cut once."

One of my more dramatic mistakes was my short partnership in what was once the largest advertising agency in the region. I joined as its president upon the death of the principal founder. I had a 10-year, no-cut contract; an option to own up to 49 percent of the business; and free rein to run the operation. In reality, as a minority owner, I was powerless to offset the misguided leadership, bad decisions, lack of vision and planning, and general confusion caused by the majority owner—the surviving spouse. Seeing only the opportunity, I failed to spend enough time up front talking with the owner about our individual goals and expectations. The company began to self-destruct and eventually put many dedicated employees out on the street. In the end my contract served only as my lever to negotiate my exit.

Ultimately, this failure became my most significant long-term learning experience. Much of what you read in this book is a product, either directly or indirectly, of that painful situation.

> **Ultimately, this failure became my most significant long-term learning experience. Much of what you read in this book is a product, either directly or indirectly, of that painful situation.**

Jon Stamell

I've repeated several times the mistake of raising false expectations among newly hired employees. Over the years, we have hired many extraordinarily bright and talented people with minimal experience. Whenever we did this, we knew we were going to throw them into the fire to see if they could survive. On several occasions, I raised expectations in people that if they could pass the test, great things awaited them. In reality, what awaited them was the steadiness of their job and more fires like the ones they had already been through. But they had been led (and by a partner) to believe there was more than this.

The net result was demands for quick promotions and higher pay from people who, in reality, had little experience. I've learned that expectations must be meted out carefully. This is particularly true if we are going to build collaborative teamwork and not nurture superstars. Ultimately, any individual needs a number of years of experience to reveal what his or her potential may be.

Personnel issues, I have found, present some of the most difficult and enduring problems managers must face. But as you will find in this book, when met head-on, the mistakes of the past serve as our lessons; personnel problems can become the opportunities that enable us to build strong and cohesive, albeit diversified, work environments.

As creative director at HHS, my past experiences, ranging from business manager to marketing consultant to copywriter, have aided my strategic ability to plot and create winning communications programs. International campaigns for countries like Chile and Norway and associations like the Norwegian Seafood Export Council and the Association of Chilean Salmon Farmers could not have had their strategic focus without my eclectic background. As a former trade show manager for some of the largest international trade shows in the marine and food industry, I learned the need not only to see vertically in an industry from consumer to manufacturer but also horizontally across industry segments to grasp the full implications of market changes. This background combining macro- and micro-views is helping me now as I strive to manage our company's rapid growth.

Melissa Field

A client was developing a project I questioned intuitively. Would the project deliver the results our client wanted? I began to question the project out loud. With irritation in his voice, the client demanded to know whether I (and the agency) was going to support his company in this project. I didn't want to ruffle feathers, so I said, "Of course we will support you." The client had knowledge and expertise in the industry, so I figured maybe his company's approach would work. Deep down, I still had doubts.

It wasn't long before I had my answer. The project failed. We lost the account. I should have listened to my inner voice and not abandoned my belief in my expertise and intuition. When challenged by the client, I should have stood my ground. When the agency was younger, I fought hard to sell and support projects I knew would work for clients. But now, since we were established and successful and had more employees relying on us for paychecks, I'm reluctant to jeopardize success and good client relations by confronting clients and perhaps losing accounts.

Well, we lost this particular account so I should have pushed. We might have saved the client wasted effort and money. We might even have saved the account. I have learned I must keep pushing when I really believe in something.

Honesty in business is about more than just telling the truth. It can mean sharing knowledge and experience a client needs in order to make the best possible decisions. In celebrating a mistake such as this, we have the opportunity to catch a potential problem early on—before it jeopardizes the business. The epiphany that follows can help us select the correct course when we're faced with the fork in the road.

My career has focused on maximizing the public relations process through the power of strategic planning. My experience isn't specific to any industry—it's diverse. And that has provided me a broad canvas from which to apply my expertise for the benefit of clients such as the Monsanto Chemical Company, Panasonic, and Yamaha Motor Corporation. The communications strategies I developed, created awareness of branded products for the Norwegian Salmon Marketing Council, Glen Ellen Winery, and Sebago. In addition, I created image campaigns for the countries of Chile and Norway, the latter as part of the 1994 Winter Olympics. As Managing Director, Communications Strategy, Worldwide, my role is to continue to build Holt, Hughes & Stamell by delivering the agency's strategic and creative intelligence to clients facing tough marketing challenges.

Honesty in business is about more than just telling the truth.

❧ ❧ ❧

In the process of learning to celebrate our own mistakes and cast off any impediments past successes might cause, we decided to write this book and share our thoughts and experiences with people in other fast-growing successful businesses. Our perspective at Holt, Hughes & Stamell is that of a midsize marketing communications company built, since 1989, on a shared vision of results-driven efforts. Our typical workdays are filled with hard work, creativity, and a healthy dose of laughter. In the pages that follow, we hope to share our vision with readers. We feel that our own search has uncovered some fairly universal truths about success and growth that virtually all companies should consider.

Celebrate Your Mistakes is a collection of our thoughts, observations, and personal experiences—the result of our newly heightened awareness. As part of our own course of self-discovery and the fact we wanted to weigh our experiences against those of others, we interviewed 12 world-class entrepreneurs, innovators, and creative forces in business. They represent industries as diverse as entertainment and finance, media

Thinking outside the box.

and marketing. For example, you will gain insight from the experiences of Julia Child; learn to keep your business on the edge from Rory Strunk; see how entrepreneur Marshall Smith focuses his vision; appreciate the drive and determination of S. Robert Levine; discover how two of the country's top investment professionals—Richard Aster and Michael Stolper—evaluate growing businesses and client relationships, respectively; and understand from Gerhard Heiberg how to bring all the lessons together.

What this book is *not* is a simple formula or series of steps guaranteed to turn your business around in a week or 10 days. Only you can do that. Rather, through *Celebrate Your Mistakes* we are sending you a wake-up call and recommending a regimen for examining and reexamining your business and its place in the worldwide market.

Now is the time for us all to look at our businesses anew, develop a fresh perspective and increased objectivity, and adopt an out-of-the-box way of thinking. The more successful we are today, the more important this process becomes. Only by remaining open to ideas and observant of the world around us can we learn to profit from the natural changes that occur in a business, in the marketplace, and in the world at large.

In the pages that follow, we want to startle and stimulate more than lecture. We hope to awaken your natural creative instincts more than prescribe a program for change. The fact is, no two companies are the same. Each has its own culture, personality, and issues, which if not unique are at least peculiar to that business. For this reason we haven't tried to etch any programs in stone for you. Nor should you expect to find success in any pre-existing formulas—even such widely heralded programs as quality circles, walk-around management, or total quality management—because there is no replacement for knowing your business, your market, and your customers, and no teacher like your own mistakes.

> **There is no replacement for knowing your business, your market, and your customers, and no teacher like your own mistakes.**

We will, however, try to rattle your cage a bit. We'll start by bombarding you with a wide range of examples of business behavior and attitudes and exploring their evolution and ramifications. This way, we hope, you'll find some companies with which to identify. You'll also realize, as we have, that some of the worst cases occur in the most successful companies. So celebrate—you're in good company.

Since it's impossible to give you a single prescription for success, we'll show you how these companies have handled their situations. Some have succeeded; others have failed. We will also provide a series of exercises designed to keep you alert to any impending failures. You can then draw your own conclusions and pick out the strategies and techniques you feel most comfortable trying. Just remember, what works for us will not necessarily be the exact solution for you.

If we have one universal lesson to give you, it is to keep your mind open to new ideas and different ways of doing what you are doing. Be willing not only to learn from your mistakes and to accept new ideas but also to toss out the old notions, which otherwise can become your personal albatross. So do what that Mariner of old could not. Rip that bird from about your neck—and any ingrained habits to boot—and get on with new business.

Our many stories, anecdotes, examples, and even a few confessions are taken from all disciplines, past and present. We selected them to demonstrate the universality of our observations and the breadth of the problems facing businesses as they prepare to enter the 21st century.

In the past year, we have developed a practiced eye for searching out the behavior that rules business decisions. You too can acquire this vision as new paradigms of thinking become second nature. But beware! When you start spotting unhealthy behavior patterns around you, and most likely in yourself as well, consider yourself cured only of the worst symptoms. This is no time to pat yourself on the back and relax. Because, like self-confessed alcoholics, we all are destined to remain in a stage of constant recovery. It's easy to slip back into old habits or develop new manifestations of our old ways. Just as a head cold can turn into pneumonia, any complacency or self-satisfaction can be the first sign of an impending reinfection. Your best prevention is to develop a new way of thinking for a lifetime. Be glad you've discovered this book. But don't ever be so glad you forget to keep one eye on your next step and the other on the horizon. Self-examination is a test you'll need to take for the rest of your life.

> **This is no time to pat yourself on the back and relax. Because, like self-confessed alcoholics, we all are destined to remain in a stage of constant recovery.**

So fasten your seat belt. You are about to embark on a journey of self-discovery. Your vantage point will be far above the maddening details of daily business decisions. Rather, you will have the opportunity to gain a new perspective, to see the whole forest rather than the trunks of a few great oaks.

We provide you with this fresh perspective with the hope you will then apply it to your own business. Later, as you turn your sights on your company, try to envision a similar distant view. Imagine, for example, your business as an Impressionist landscape painting by Claude Monet or Auguste Renoir. Perhaps this will force you to stand back and appreciate the whole picture.

As you prepare for your journey, be sure to take your flight bag, because along the way we'll summarize some of the key points you should pack away for future use. And remember, this is a voyage of never-ending discovery. Just as you must never stop celebrating your mistakes, you must keep right on course.

"All good drama has two movements," wrote the 20th-century American poet W. H. Auden, "first the making of the mistake, then the discovery that it was a mistake." Let's celebrate the drama of our mistakes, and use that discovery to make our companies even smarter and more successful.

CHAPTER 1

The Pollyanna Syndrome

"To him whose elastic and vigorous thought keeps pace with the sun, the day is a perpetual morning."
—Henry David Thoreau

"In any profession, you learn something new almost every day. So if you aren't learning something new every day, you're practically dead."

—Julia Child on not being lulled to sleep by success

Textbook Signs of Illness

In cataloging the problem we address in this book, we have been very careful to describe the condition as the *Pollyanna syndrome*. We are not suggesting that U.S. corporations and entrepreneurial ventures are diseased and sick. Rather, we have diagnosed a set of ailments—and rather varied and nonspecific ones at that—that prey most aggressively on once-healthy companies, which in this case represent some of the most successful businesses in the country. We call the condition a syndrome for the simple fact that, in medical parlance, a syndrome—while all too real—is often difficult to diagnose. Doctors use the word *syndrome* to refer to a pattern of symptoms and complaints that collectively suggest or indicate the presence of a particular ailment. It is just such a pattern of characteristic symptoms that we outline in the pages that follow.

> **"In any profession, you learn something new almost every day. So if you aren't learning something new every day, you're practically dead."**
>
> *—Julia Child on not being lulled to sleep by success*

The word *Pollyanna* has crept into our common language. The *Oxford English Dictionary* defines Pollyanna as "one who is unduly optimistic or achieves happiness through self-delusion." The word springs from Eleanor Porter's 1913 children's classic in which the flaxen-haired orphaned daughter of missionaries teaches a small eastern town the "just being glad" game. "You see," Pollyanna explains, "when you're hunting for the glad things, you sort of forget the other kind." While this was a wonderful game for a naive young girl growing up in a simpler time who needed a way to cope with personal hardships, it's not for the entrepreneur preparing to enter the 21st century.

But what has this little girl to do with you or your company? Actually, a popular magazine established the connection as early as 1921 when an editor wrote, "I should not like to hold stock in a company with Pollyanna as president," a comment remarkably prescient, given the 1929 stock-market crash and its aftermath. You see, those infected with the Pollyanna syndrome become eternal optimists who expect everything to be right, even as the sky is falling around their shoulders. By our definition, they often are blinded by their own previous success. Other times they are scared to death to know what is really going on in their market. If they ever looked outside their office, talked with customers, or shopped the competition, they might be forced to change. And that scares the hell out of them, so they remain wedded to their ignorance. Content in their isolation, they tell themselves it isn't necessary to do anything because things are fine. Even in the best companies, owners and top management have a tendency to work very hard to get to a point where they believe they can sit on the crest of the selling wave and just ride it for years and years. This book, then, is dedicated to shaking up the Pollyanna in all of us.

The fact is, the Pollyanna syndrome is probably as old as commerce itself. Stories abound of failure following in the footsteps of success. The New England ice industry, for example, collapsed just a few short years after reaching its apex. In 1806, a young Boston merchant, Frederick "Ice King" Tudor, sent his first load of ice to Cuba. He got the idea for exporting New England's ice after hearing the stories of lumber shipped from New England in winter and arriving in the West Indies weeks later still covered with ice. Tudor hired men to chop and store Massachusetts ice, which he then placed in insulated ships and sent to ports in the southern United States, the Caribbean, and South America. By the 1830s, he was transporting his ice as far away as India, a voyage of more than four months.

But even as the ice industry grew, new refrigeration technology was developing. In 1842, when a shipment of Maine ice failed to arrive in Florida, a physician, John Gorrie, desperate to find some way to cool down the room where his sick wife lay in bed, devised a method of artificial refrigeration using a bucket full of ammonia that evaporated as it dripped. In 1867 French inventor Ferdinand Carre demonstrated his method for manufacturing artificial ice using a liquid ammonia compressor to produce six tons of ice daily at the French Industrial Exposition.

Yet natural ice harvesting moved forward in virtual lockstep with artificial ice manufacturing. Ice exports to tropical ports reached its height in 1880 when 1,735 ships carried almost 900,000 tons of ice. By 1886, U.S. companies were harvesting 25 million tons of ice annually, much of which came from Maine's Kennebec River, whose ice was prized for its density, clarity, and good taste. Over a period of about 50 years, commercial ice harvesting and exporting thrived, employing thousands of people. Ice enabled people to brew beer in summer, to better preserve meat, and to transport fresh fruits and vegetables farther from the fields. Although the methods changed little in all that time, resulting in as much as 40 percent of the ice melting in transit, the profits were great, and many people grew rich.

We would expect the ice harvesters to see the potential for new technology. But because natural ice was cheap and abundant, they ignored the warning signs. Not even the warm winters of 1880 and 1889 deterred New England's ice magnates. Nor did the fact that by 1894 ice-making plants were producing 1.5 million tons of machine-made ice.

Almost as quickly as it started, the demand for natural ice disappeared. By the turn of the century, the industry was in decline. Only World War I gave the failing industry a brief reprieve, since citizens were encouraged to rely on natural resources and reserve chemicals like ammonia for the war effort. But by the early 1920s, large-scale ice harvesting had virtually vanished. Ice harvesters, shippers, storage houses, and ice wagons were out of business. Even among the dozens of ice-box manufacturers, very few moved into the electric refrigeration business—apparent victims of the Pollyanna syndrome.

> **Market taste is a moving, breathing, living organism. To be successful—and remain so—at the very least you have to be prepared to chase the movement.**

There was a saying in the 60s, "I know where it's at," which was people's way of saying they were cool and "with it." As a joke, someone created a bumper sticker that was a play on this phrase. It read, "Just when I think I know where it's at, they move it." Few one-liners better describe the fickle, ever-changing nature of the marketplace, and the problem of marketing and selling to it. Market taste is a moving, breathing, living organism. To be successful—and remain so—at the very least you have to be prepared to chase the movement. Ideally you should figure out where the market is going before "they move it" or, better still, discover how you can make the market want to chase you.

One of the great misconceptions of those suffering the Pollyanna syndrome, however, is their tendency to believe the market they have today will remain loyal forever. But if this were the case, the landscape

Of Mice and Men . . . and Old Dogs

They say you can't teach an old dog new tricks. How often have you found yourself shying away from something new and different? Consider the meat-and-potatoes gourmand who's afraid to try sushi. Or the crusty old reporter who won't give up that battered Underwood manual typewriter. We all have our prejudices and fears.

Take the person down the hall who learned word processing in the dark ages of the 1980s and refuses to switch to one of the newer programs complete with graphical point-and-click interface and mouse. Many touch typists have remained skeptical and still argue that it is better to keep both hands on the keyboard than to go reaching for the mouse every time they want to edit or move about the screen. While there is some merit to their position, their rigidity has prevented them from using some of the most advanced personal computer software available today. This is a perfect example of not being willing to unlearn ingrained habits. You don't have to embrace every new technology or trend to come along, but at least remain open to the possibilities.

of companies serving our every need would look a lot different than it does now. The names of successful corporations today would match those of generations past. Consider the following hypothetical scenario:

It's five o'clock, Friday afternoon, on a warm July day. Joe leaves his job at U.S. Steel in Pittsburgh, Pennsylvania, and heads home. He is driving his late-model red DeSoto with the top down and the Atwater Kent radio blaring.

Joe arrives home and has a home cooked dinner with his family. Afterwards, he opens the Kelvinator and takes out an ice-cold Piel's. He heads for the den and turns on the Philco to watch a St. Louis Browns baseball game while he eats his meal. He kicks off his favorite pair of Red Ball Jets before stretching out on the couch. For dessert, Joe practically inhales a heaping bowl full of Howard Johnson's ice cream—his favorite.

Far from being the market leaders as described in this little scenario, most of these companies are now extinct. And those that aren't certainly do not have the market share or national presence today they might have enjoyed. Yet each company once had either a prominent national brand or a large regional customer base from which to grow.

Why today do we drive Jeeps and minivans, Saabs and Lexuses instead of DeSotos and Studebakers? Why do we watch Mitsubishi 20-inch color televisions and wear Nikes and Reeboks? Why do we seek out the new microbrewery beers, flavored waters, and bottled ice teas rather than drink the same beers as our fathers and grandfathers?

> **There is no single answer to why companies fail or miss opportunities. Every business has its own story to tell.**

There is no single answer to why companies fail or miss opportunities. Every business has its own story to tell Still, we can generalize a little and give you six basic reasons why companies lose market share, which also happen to describe six examples of what we call classic Pollyanna behavior. Quite simply, Pollyannas:

1. Fail to listen to their customers and employees.
2. Fail to act on changes and trends in markets and in technology.
3. Fail to keep at least one eye on the competition, including potential encroachment from other sectors.
4. Fail to encourage risk and divergent opinions among employees.
5. Fail to take an inclusive approach to problem solving.
6. Fail to believe that their company could ever fail.

These six failures have one thing in common: All are exacerbated by complacency brought on by success. Polaroid, for example, the company that revolutionized amateur photography in the 1950s with its instant cameras, may have committed all six failures. Recently it has had four years of flat earnings, culminating in a $32 million loss for the first quarter of 1995. Yet instant photography, 90 percent of Polaroid's business, is not only growing at the rate of 4 percent a year but is projected to increase in the next few years, and film sales have a high profit margin.

In its success may lie the seeds of Polaroid's problems: a success that built a rigid corporate culture so engrained that even insiders admit the company has talked more than it has listened to customers and employees. A success that, when performance declined, made Polaroid a prime target for a takeover that cost $400 million to fend off. A success that made the company slow to address some serious distribution and retail problems.

Management and investment analyst reports suggest that Polaroid is changing. It has reengineered its internal systems, cleaned up distribution and retail problems, and developed electronic-imaging technology to take the company into the 21st century. Today Polaroid's employees are freer to initiate changes, and an employee stock option program is giving people a stake in the business.

But while these changes suggest Polaroid has cast off the mantle of Pollyanna, they don't explain the OneStep talking camera. It's not designed to add sound to still imagery but rather to record the photographer's voice saying something silly to catch the subject off guard and get a funny expression or a smile. The photographer records his or her voice prior to snapping the picture, then the camera repeats it back just as the picture is taken. For example, you might record something like "Oh, look, there's Halley's comet," or "Smile, Big Brother is watching." Anything goes. We feel this is more a marketing gimmick than an evolutionary, let alone revolutionary, step from a company once respected for its innovation.

On the front page of the April 7, 1995, *The Wall Street Journal,* Dana Milbank detailed the story of the London cabby.* In his traditional black cab, he is feeling strong competition from the independent minicabs—unregulated and unsupervised—that are springing up all over the city. Rather than compete head-to-head, the London cabby remains isolated from the realities of the marketplace, in large part due to a 350-year heritage dominated by the era of the horse-drawn hack. By law, for example, London's black cabs must be tall enough so that a gentleman need not remove his top hat while sitting; the trunk must be of a size and volume to accommodate a bale of hay; and any cabby is permitted to turn down trips to locations more than six miles from town because old regulations state that this is too far for the horses that used to pull carriages to travel. Before they are licensed, London black-cab drivers must train for three to four years, during which time they must acquire "The Knowledge"—they must know not only every street in London but also the exact locations of major restaurants, theaters, and other points of interest. Minicabs, on the other hand, are unregulated. They can set their own fees, which can sometimes catch off guard the unsuspecting tourist traveling any distance from town.

---

*Dana Milbank, "The London Taxi May Go the Way of the London Bridge," *The Wall Street Journal,* Section A: p. 1, Column 4.

Who's to blame for the plight of the London cabby? In this case, the blame is probably fairly evenly spread between the government, which regulates, and the cabbies, who haven't fought harder for change. In fact, some London black-cab drivers have retreated complacently into their tradition. As a result, today there are more than 40,000 minicabs and only about half as many black cabs, suggesting that unless some changes are made, the London black cab may be traveling the road to extinction.

You see how easily successful entrepreneurs can turn into Pollyannas. They convince themselves they are infallible and above the realities of the marketplace. Resting on past laurels, they demand that their sales force sell what they manufacture—regardless of whether the market has changed. They believe the right advertising will sprinkle products with magic dust and move them off the shelves. And so it is that smart companies can go down the wrong path.

> **The reality that virtually all Pollyannas are missing is that change is the only constant.**

The reality that virtually all Pollyannas are missing is that change is the only constant. Admittedly this concept is easier to accept in theory than in practice. The truth is, we don't know anyone, including ourselves, who really enjoys grabbing the proverbial bootstraps and reinventing themselves again and again. But in today's technology-driven global marketplace, there are but two positions: We either move forward or stagnate. In our environment, change and risk taking, which is part of change, are essential to survival. The failures that will accompany some of your attempts at change are just part of the process, so recognize them for what they are—part of the learning curve—and act accordingly. You'll come out ahead. Do we sound too certain? Perhaps this is because as business owners ourselves, we too have faced the vagaries of the Pollyanna syndrome.

We're Not Pollyannas . . . Anymore

At Holt, Hughes & Stamell, thinking we had performed our job well, especially given our efforts to bestow greater independence and opportunity on junior staff, we gradually were lulled into a state of complacency. Did we have problems? "Sure, but who doesn't? We'll work them out," we

What's Your Pollyanna Index?

The following list includes some typical Pollyannaish remarks. If you recognize yourself or others saying two or more of these statements, look out, you're a budding Pollyanna. If you've uttered more than five of these remarks, you are a full-fledged member of the club. We'll warn you now, the list is quite inclusive—illustrating how pervasive the symptoms are. But as you continue through this book, you will find the antidotes you will need to fight off the Pollyanna syndrome.

- We own this market.
- We started this trend.
- We tried that before.
- We'll know change when we see it.
- Our business is unlike any you've ever seen.
- Of course we are prepared for the future; we have a 10-year plan.
- We have brand equity and our customers are very loyal.
- We deal with retail store owners, so we don't need a customer database.
- We just hired you to do the ads; don't tell us our business.
- My children are going to run this business; this is a family business. We don't hire outsiders.
- Only 10 percent of our customers will ever use that function.
- If only 5 percent of our customers don't like us, we don't worry about it.
- It's not that we need more customers; we just need our customers to use us more often.
- Total quality is everything.
- I don't worry about customer issues; that's why I have a sales manager.
- My door is always open; people just don't seem to come in.
- We know what our customer wants, and that's what we make.
- We'll make it up in volume.
- This company has made the same thing for 50 years. That's what we do now, and that's what we're always going to do. That's what people know us for.

said. "We'll be able to discuss them." But the truth was, it wasn't happening, and our organization wasn't going anywhere. People on our account teams had trouble taking the lead in being self-directed. Because individuals weren't comfortable grabbing responsibility, teams tended to turn into work groups headed by a supervisor. At the same time, we weren't providing direction or leadership. We had pulled back deliberately in an effort to avoid that most distasteful of conditions—top-down management.

The irony for us was that we thought we were staying attuned to the needs of both our employees and our clients. The proof of our success, we felt, was in our growth. We were becoming self-satisfied, while trying to prepare our junior people for greater responsibility. Some real fissures were developing. In fact, we were Pollyannas in training.

> **The proof of our success, we felt, was in our growth. We were becoming self-satisfied, while trying to prepare our junior people for greater responsibility. Some real fissures were developing.**

Gradually we realized what was happening. We saw little problems popping up one right after another. We were winning new business based on work—good work—that was more than a year old. This, we suggest, is a warning sign: When you are more proud of work you did a year ago than the work you are doing today, an alarm bell should go off. Clients also began telling us there were little problems on their accounts. Finally, a client from Norway said, "I understand what you people are doing. You want to pull back and let other people grow. But there's a gap between what you know and what they know. They haven't been able to fill it. Either you have to hire people who, through some combination of experience and talent, are able to challenge clients to do their best or you have to come back and work with me on a day-to-day basis." This client was convinced we got more out of him when we challenged him and created an environment for bouncing ideas around.

This conversation was our epiphany—or perhaps nadir is a better word. We decided to act quickly and decisively to involve the entire staff in the restructuring process. We felt sure they would have some real insight into our problems, and we were right. In January, we sent out the following companywide memo:

MEMO
───

To: Holt, Hughes & Stamell Staff
From: Jon, John, George
Re: Maintaining an edge

While the end of our fiscal year is still a month away, the year so far has been a good one for all of us—our sixth year of continuous growth. Those of you who were here a year ago will recall being in an office space one-third this size. And if you were here four years ago, you'll remember the modified dorm rooms from which this company began. Your personal perspective of this company starts with the size and corporate culture that existed on your first day of work. If you're starting here today, or for those starting over the next few weeks, your first image will be drastically different from those of you who began on Fore Street.

At the same time, as we reflect on our success, we believe we should express some concerns about its impact. To paraphrase an old adage, Whom the gods want to destroy, they send years of success. We don't think destruction is imminent, but we see some signs that suggest a lessening of focus and energy and signs of complacency. This is not an attempt to point fingers unless it's at the overall feeling of the agency. We think the signs are subtle but here nonetheless, and this is the time to do something about it.

We asked every member of the staff to join us in the job of "remaking" the agency by reexamining the way we work, questioning our approach, making changes, and institutionalizing risk. In addition to having the account teams brainstorm, we asked each individual to submit written answers to four questions:

1. Describe your job a year from now. Two years from now.
2. What risks are you going to take this year?
3. How are you going to be entrepreneurial this year?
4. Write something about this company that no one else knows.

As you might expect, when we gathered the staff together, they harbored some natural skepticism and, more important, real concern that we were creating more work for them to cram their already-busy schedules.

But as they began to work on their answers, they saw the importance of the task. Since then, everyone has taken our "No Pollyannas" process seriously. Our staff gave freely of their advice and recommendations for restructuring jobs and departments: "Spread the brainpower around a bit and erase territorial lines . . . eliminate, or reevaluate, all titles on business cards." Another example: "Periodic exercise for the staff (mind games) at the Thursday morning meetings." And: "Let go of perceived organizational/personal limitations and judgments."

Our staff's responses to the questions varied widely, but virtually all were constructive—reason enough for us to recommend this exercise to you. The responses have given us a better understanding of both the ambitions and frustrations of each employee. Each of the exercises we suggest on the pages that follow are the result of real-life efforts we have made and continue to make in order to keep Pollyannas from developing within our company. We emphasize the word *continue* because this is a program for life.

In the months that have followed, we have enjoyed many little indicators that suggest we are probably on the right path as we proceed on a never-ending journey of reinvention. For example, one of our employees, en route home from a client site outside the United States, was concerned about our efforts on that account and sent the following E-mail to the entire staff:

> We're facing some challenges . . . that personality and cultural differences compound. They're not going away. Let's take a first step to productivity and reflect on how we relate and communicate with our client. Please take your time and stew on the following questions I asked myself homeward bound . . . Then let's discuss as a group ASAP to determine how we are going to overcome these differences and challenges and get to work in a way that is both productive and fulfilling.

Among her questions were the following: Do we listen and then address concerns? Do we patronize? Do we not ask for client input and support enough? Do we focus more on process than results? Do we talk more than listen? Do we insist we're right when sometimes it doesn't really matter? In spite of these very real issues, we felt that the mere fact that she felt not only concerned but also secure enough to pose such questions was a good sign for the future of our firm.

Six Exercises for Budding Pollyannas

Here, in a nutshell, are the six critical exercises on which you need to focus. You can apply your own brand of creativity to tackling each. Some of the more specific exercises included in this book will help you explore one or more of these areas further.

1. Reexamine the premise of your business. It has changed.
2. Expose yourself and avoid the culture of insulation.
3. Defy the corporate culture. Institutionalize risk.
4. Imagine the world without your product. Why will it happen?
5. Assume everything you have done has failed. Now reinvent yourself.
6. Compete against yourself.

Success and Other Sins

"Whom the gods wish to destroy, they send 40 years of success," wrote Peter Drucker in a 1993 article for *The Wall Street Journal*. Although the origin of this adage (which we modified for our wake-up memo to our staff) appears to be Herodotus—"Whom the gods wished to destroy, they first made mad"—over the years "success" appears to have supplanted "anger" as the source of our destruction. There's no limit to the references and warnings about the perils of too much success and its power to destroy. Philosophers, teachers, theologians, and novelists have all expressed this relationship between success and ultimate destruction.

We warned you at the outset that there was no simple formula we could impart except to help you find your own path. There is, however, one universal rule we can share, a rule that is as hard to live by as it is critical: Don't allow your past success to become a screen through which you filter all your new experiences. In other words, don't try to model your future success on the past.

"Someday son, this will all be yours."

When we are looking to invest in mutual funds, we are reminded in the small print that past history is no guarantee of future success. In fact, this applies to any business. "Yet we tend to get vested in belief systems [that] to a large extent, represent pattern recognition," explains Michael Stolper, who spends much of his time evaluating people and investment vehicles. "[In the case of] things that yielded success in the past, there is a presumption that they'll succeed in the future."

Stolper tells of the experiences of a friend: "I know a very successful businessman who has hired a lot of people. He says they will always repeat whatever they did that was clever in their previous lives. There is always this presumption that they found something formulaic. [They want] to repeat success in essentially the same way throughout their whole lives . . . to replicate in as close a fashion as they can, to engineer the same phenomenon . . . I think my friend's cynical view is that

The Trouble with Success

"His success may be great, but be it ever so great the wheel of fortune may turn again and bring him down in the dust."
—The Buddah: *His Life and Teachings* (500 B.C.)

"The secret of this was their general extraordinary success, which made them confuse their success with their hopes."
—Thucydides, *History of the Peloponnesian War* (431 B.C.)

"Success throws a shade on all his odious qualities (for nothing veils men's faults from observation so effectually as success): but let any accident happen, and they will all be perfectly discovered."
—Demosthenes, *The Oration on the Letter* (Philip's Letter to the Athenians, 339, B.C.)

". . . and gloriously routing the enemy, followed the pursuit, in the pride and exultation of success, so eagerly, and so unwisely, that it fatally lost him the day."
—Plutarch, *Demetrius* (A.D. 75)

"Hitherto, you have only borne adversity; prosperity tries the heart with keener temptations; for hardships may be endured, whereas we are spoiled by success."
—P. Cornelius Tacitus, *Histories* (A.D. 96)

"The greater their success the worse it proves."
—Lord Byron, *Don Juan* (1819–24)

"Carried away by his success, he forgot where he was."
—Stendhal, *The Red and the Black* (1830)

". . . because he had tasted for the first time Responsibility and Success. Those two make an intoxicating drink, and have ruined more men than ever has Whiskey."
—Rudyard Kipling, *His Chance in Life* (1888)

"You are fat with power and possession, drunken with success."
—Jack London, *Iron Heel* (1907)

"The gods do not love success unless it comes by accident."
—John Steinbeck, *The Pearl* (1947)

most people have limited utility, they will do one or two things right in their lives and then spend the rest of their lives trying to repeat, [changing only] on the margin . . . It's just a human condition that we're resistant to change. [Imbuing] companies with a corporate policy of obsolescing their own products at intervals—that is a very courageous posture."

If you doubt the power of success to reverse our fortunes, consider how the Fortune 500 list has changed over the past 40 years. When we compare the top-25 list from the 1954 "Fortune Directory," (published in 1955, the first year *Fortune* magazine ranked the top 500 industrial corporations) with the 1989 and 1994 top-25 lists, we find some dramatic shifts:

Rank	1954	1989	1994
1	General Motors	General Motors	General Motors
2	Standard Oil of NJ	Ford Motor	Ford Motor
3	*U.S. Steel (45)*	Exxon	Exxon
4	General Electric	IBM	Wal-Mart Stores
5	*Swift*	General Electric	AT&T
6	Chrysler	Mobil	General Electric
7	*Armour*	Philip Morris	IBM
8	*Gulf Oil*	Chrysler	Mobil
9	*Socony-Vacuum Oil*	E.I. Du Pont	Sears Roebuck
10	E.I. Du Pont	Texaco	Philip Morris
11	*Bethlehem Steel (239)*	Chevron	Chrysler
12	Standard Oil (Ind.)	Amoco	State Farm Group
13	*Westinghouse Electric (121)*	Shell Oil	Prudential Insurance
14	Texas Co.	Procter & Gamble	E.I. Du Pont
15	*Western Electric*	Boeing	Kmart
16	*Shell Oil*	Occidental Petroleum	Texaco
17	*National Dairy Products*	United Technologies	Citicorp
18	Standard Oil of Calif.	Eastman Kodak	Chevron
19	*Goodyear Tire & Rubber (81)*	USX	Procter & Gamble
20	*Boeing Airplane (29)*	Dow Chemical	Pepsico
21	*Sinclair Oil*	Xerox	Amoco
22	*International Harvester*	Atlantic Richfield	Hewlett-Packard
23	*Radio Corporation of America*	Pepsico	ITT
24	*Union Carbide & Carbon (236)*	RJR Nabisco	Conagra
25	*Firestone Tire & Rubber*	McDonnell Douglas	Kroger

Compiled from *Fortune* magazines, April 1955, April 1990, April 1995.

Note that the 17 companies in the first column (1954) that are in italics are no longer in the top 25. In fact, most are no longer on the Fortune 500 list, due either to consolidation, buyout, or having gone out of business; six moved farther down the list.

While it's true that General Motors was number one back in 1954 and still occupies that position today, even General Motors does not command the power and unwavering respect it once did. Who today would agree with former CEO Charles Wilson's 1952 remark before the Senate Armed Forces Committee: "What's good for the country is good for General Motors, and what's good for General Motors is good for the country?"

The most obvious change in the past 40 years is the decline of steel manufacturers and heavy industry. In 1954, seven steel manufacturers ranked in the top 100. Today, we find USX in the 45th position. The former U.S. Steel was number 3 in 1954, and Bethlehem Steel (once in the number 11 spot) has dropped to the 239th position. Most of the others are gone. Their replacements read like a who's who of Silicon Valley. The Fortune 500 is going high-tech as the knowledge-intensive industries increasingly replace the heavy industrials. Today's list includes five computer and data services companies; 13 computer and office equipment manufacturers; 17 electronics and electrical suppliers; 14 telecommunications companies; and eight scientific, photo, and control equipment manufacturers—most of which did not even exist in 1954.

For the same reasons, we find many more publishing, printing, and news-service companies on the list: R.R. Donnelley and Sons, Times Mirror, Gannett, Reader's Digest Association, McGraw-Hill, Knight-Ridder, and the New York Times are all Fortune 500 companies. Only Time Inc. (now Time Warner) and Times Mirror made the 1954 list.

The other obvious change is the increase in consumer product manufacturers and merchandisers: 20 specialty retailers, 21 food producers, 13 general merchandisers, 23 food and drug stores, four beverage companies, four soap and cosmetic developers, three apparel companies, and two toy manufacturers. We are a country of consumers, and our behavior is reflected in the Fortune 500.

Thanks to the pace of change brought on by market trends, global exposure, new technology, and the existence of more entrepreneurs, we can be certain that the rate of turnover will continue. Regardless of your size, if you are not changing with the times, you are in danger of joining the ranks of the permanently failed.

Having said that, we should add that our definition of failure and Pollyannaism includes not only companies that have gone out of business—the dinosaurs of our market-driven society—but also those that have missed opportunities and not achieved their potential. By our yardstick, these companies have failed almost as badly as the bankrupt and out-of-business companies. We're talking about the Pollyannas who aren't necessarily looking at the world through the rose-colored glasses of eternal optimism but rather wearing horse blinders. It's often only a matter of time before many of them also will be extinct. Stop and think of a few examples, for we all know companies that continue to exist and manage to get by somehow—sometimes just because of sheer momentum. One example that comes to mind is the five-and-dime store.

The Death of the Five-and-Dime—Was It Mass Murder or Suicide?

Not so many years ago, the five-and-dime store, also called the variety store, was an American institution. Ben Franklin, W. T. Grant, J. J. Newberry, McCrory, and, of course, F. W. Woolworth dotted every Main Street in America. When you stop to realize how completely the good, old-fashioned variety store has disappeared, you have to ask, Was it mass murder or suicide? Or simply because nothing today sells for five cents? The answer has to be, They killed themselves, although not deliberately, for most certainly the world has not stopped buying what these variety stores once sold.

The 10 Largest U.S. Retailers: A 20-Year View

Rank	1973	1983	1993
1	Sears, Roebuck	Sears, Roebuck	Wal-Mart Stores
2	Safeway Stores	Kmart	Sears, Roebuck
3	Great Atlantic & Pacific Tea	Safeway Stores	Kmart
4	J. C. Penney	Kroger	Kroger
5	S. S. Kresge	J. C. Penney	J. C. Penney
6	Kroger	Southland	Dayton Hudson
7	Marcor	Federated Department Stores	American Stores
8	F. W. Woolworth	Lucky Stores	Safeway Stores
9	Federated Department Stores	American Stores	Albertson's
10	Rapid-American	Household International	May Department Stores

Source: Hoover's Database (on-line), originally from *Fortune*, annual list issues, 1974–1994.

Frank Winfield Woolworth opened his first store in 1879. At the time of his death, in 1919, he owned more than 1,000 stores. The business continued to grow throughout the roaring 20s, the depressed 30s, and the patriotic 40s. In fact, it's really only been in the last 20 years that the variety store has faded from our midst. By 1973, Woolworth had fallen to the eighth position among the country's largest retailers. Within a few years, it wouldn't even make the top 10, and in recent years has closed more than 1,000 stores. How could such a mighty empire crumble? While the reasons are many—too much variety, very low-end product line, no distinguishing niche, wrong geography—it all comes down to a change in shopping patterns brought on largely by the automobile.

The trend five-and-dime stores missed was that Americans left the variety store on Main Street for specialty stores in the shopping mall and the discount department stores carrying brand-name products at the lowest prices. As we said, Americans never stopped needing the items variety stores carried. They just went elsewhere to get them. There was still room for variety; stores just needed to figure out how to make it work. They needed, for example, to rein in the amount of inventory, move their locations to malls, raise quality, and buy in large enough volume to discount the items people wanted most. This was the formula the five-and-dime store couldn't comprehend. The difference was one of emphasis: Whereas Woolworth and others focused on the variety, Wal-Mart and Kmart focused on value.

Woolworth tried to break into the value discount-store niche with its Woolco stores, but it was more of an extension than a repositioning. Woolworth stores didn't disappear; Woolco stores just joined them. Having enjoyed success for so many years, the Woolworth chain seemingly could not break the variety-store image or mentality.

The Woolworth Corporation, on the other hand, has made the transition. Through a series of acquisitions, it has moved successfully into the mall. Its Kinney Shoes and Foot Locker stores, to name two of its most popular subsidiaries, are a powerful presence. The variety stores, however, remained such inveterate Pollyannas they may well have committed all six of the failures listed on p. 6. Apparently unable or unwilling to see the trend, Woolworth's was slow to leave Main Street and unprepared to cut and redefine its inventory. In short, it could not change with the times and believed its customer base—the shopper on Main Street—not only would stay loyal but also would continue to shop downtown.

Only one variety-store chain, S. S. Kresge, recognized the trend and responded accordingly. Kresge not only made the transition by recasting itself as Kmart but did it so radically that the company went from the number five position as Kresge in 1973 to the number two position as Kmart, right behind Sears, by 1983. It fell to the number three slot in the 1990s because Wal-Mart shot to the head of the list. But even such a successful transition has not left Kmart immune to the Pollyanna syndrome. In its most recent annual report, Kmart managers acknowledged their failures—among them, the tendency toward companywide edicts coming from the central offices in Troy, Michigan, that made it difficult for individual stores to respond to retail changes and demographic shifts in their communities. They also described the steps they are taking to turn the company around: more emphasis on name brands, wider variety of the most popular items, better stocked shelves, and more marketing.

We can't examine the failure of the five-and-dime store without looking at the all-around retail winner—Wal-Mart. Many who know only of Sam Walton's success consider him a genius. But those who knew the man speak of his penchant for hard work and his serious devotion to the marketplace. The complete antithesis of a Pollyanna, Walton was ever alert to customers and competition. He also was willing to experiment and take chances. Even after his initial success, he avoided the trap of complacency and remained quick to pick up on new trends. When cash-and-carry warehouse shopping began to capture the customers' interest, Walton started a chain of Sam's Club warehouses, which have done very well. Sam Walton was always on the move—visiting his stores, talking with and listening to his employees and customers, and checking out the other stores in town.

Since Walton's death, 19 regional vice presidents make the circuit each week, visiting each of the stores and essentially doing what the boss used to do. It's too early to tell, however, whether they can both sustain Walton's innovations and risk-taking nature and build on his legacy. Will success ultimately turn Wal-Mart's management into cautious Pollyannas? We can only watch and wait. An interesting twist on the outcome is that Wal-Mart recently purchased Woolworth Corporation's 120 Woolco stores throughout Canada. The company saw Woolworth's established presence there as an easy way to enter that market.

Gain a Fresh Perspective

Any individual or organization can benefit from gaining a fresh perspective—even government. Today, a fresh new breeze is blowing through the statehouse in Augusta. Maine's governor, Angus King, is currently the only independent governor in the country, and his impact on business-as-usual has been interesting to watch. Because he lacks a party affiliation, he is not bound to appoint the usual cast of party supporters and hangers-on. And as an independent he has no prescribed party agenda.

King's primary objective is to whip things into shape by establishing better lines of communication. He's not an old pol; he's a businessman with a businessman's concerns. The state house in Augusta is his boardroom, and he's filling it with appointments whose perspectives are fresh and quite varied. He's putting Democrats and Republicans in the same room with Independents, businesspeople, and academicians. Hardly a Pollyanna, Angus King is willing to open the windows to new horizons.

Angus King was a lawyer for many years and was on his way to becoming an established player in the traditional political party system when he suddenly left the legal profession to create Northeast Energy Management. The company helps private industry institute energy conservation changes that are resulting in direct savings to their bottom lines. He sold the company in 1994, netting $8 million in profits.

Before taking office, the then Governor-Elect King gave a speech to University of Maine graduates that, instead of being filled with broad platitudes, was light, slightly offbeat, and reflected his different point of view. He substituted the traditional agenda-setting remarks with a commentary on common sense, basic values, and good advice. He gave the graduates a list of 13 real-world, practical tips they should take forward with them in life—13 ways, we would say, to avoid becoming a Pollyanna.

Governor King's Advice to the University of Maine Graduating Class

1. Take more chances with your future.
2. Don't limit yourself.
3. Don't be afraid to make mistakes. If you're not making mistakes, you're not trying hard enough.
4. Listen to yourself and don't take your cues from others.
5. Learn to write an outline. Figure out how to say things in a logical way and go forward.

6. Be honest even when it hurts.

7. Treat each job and task as if it's the most important you've ever had.

8. Value each day and take advantage of what life gives you, and don't waste a lot of time worrying.

9. Don't look for happiness in places and things. Happiness is in your head.

10. Value friends and never let them down.

11. Believe in something.

12. Always round off the cents in your checkbook to the nearest dollar. It will save aggravation and addition and subtraction.

13. Always have $10 tucked away. The day will come when you will need it.

The bottom line is that Angus King has decided not to be driven by the past—the years of success and affluence in this country that have contributed to the hidebound government we endure today. Rather, Governor King has taken his commonsense notions from business and applied them to government—a task with as many frustrations as rewards. King had been in office about eight months when we asked him to discuss his experiences and assess his impact. The following are a few excerpts from that conversation.

Authors: What's the biggest surprise you've had since coming to office?

King: I think one big surprise is the vitality and power of sheer partisanship. Decisions quite often are influenced by other than what are the merits of the proposition at hand, and are really questions of politics . . . the dynamic pushes you toward confrontation rather than cooperation.

Authors: What are some of the differences between running a business and running the government here in Maine?

King: In the business sector quite often decisions are taken somewhat arbitrarily and without sufficient compilation. Around here everything is compilation, and you really learn to build consensus and to do everything necessary to include people and get them to buy in to a solution. Quite often in the business world . . . you end up with a leader going in one direction and the workers being mad or the customers being mad. There's sometimes a lack of communication that here [in government] is utterly necessary. If I can't communicate and work with the legislators or the press or the public, I can't do anything.

The purpose of a management organization and a business is efficiency. And efficiency is defined as the extent to which you can make decisions and have them implemented . . . I'm trying to bring in a sense of vision, but I'm also trying to bring a sense of management, which is tricky.

> **Quite often in the business world . . . you end up with a leader going in one direction and the workers being mad or the customers being mad.**

Authors: By the same token, what parallels do you find?

King: I'm an absolute believer that there is something in the world called leadership . . . One of the essential qualities of leadership is being able to ask the right question . . . I never thought of that before as a part of the package that a leader should have, but I can't go out and run a Department of Human Services. Therefore, I need to be able to ask the commissioner the right questions to be sure that he or she is running the department properly . . . I think that's part of leadership, hiring the right people and knowing what your own limitations are.

Authors: Independence can work to one's advantage in business. What pluses does it offer in government?

King: We were able to get from the legislature this past session several items that I don't believe a partisan governor could have gotten. One is the line-item veto . . . There were other areas where I could be sort of a broker where the parties had differences and we could come in and broker the middle ground . . .

We really tried to maintain a civil tone and to talk to each other, to communicate. I had, I'm told by other people, an unprecedented amount of contact with the legislators . . .

By and large, not knowing the rules is positive because you're not bound by the constraints.

Far from frustrated, King is enjoying his new experience, which he likens to "an actor who is doing Hamlet twice a day and writing the

Move outside the Box

Can you ever imagine the typical Pollyanna board member asking an assembly-line worker, "How do you think we should do things"? An extreme example? Perhaps. We're not advocating a boardroom full of assembly-line workers, only trying to rattle your cage a little and encourage you to see things through the eyes of others—customers, noncustomers, former customers, and other employees.

Just as Governor King said, "not knowing the rules is positive because you're not bound by the constraints." We can all benefit from freeing our minds to fresh thinking. We want you to develop an out-of-the-box attitude. Come up with new ways to get ideas and information. If that means, in part, asking the guys down on the loading dock, so be it.

Here's a little brain teaser you may remember from your childhood. Draw nine dots on a piece of paper in a pattern like this:

```
        •       •       •


        •       •       •


        •       •       •
```

Now, without lifting your pencil, connect all nine dots with just four straight lines. Remember how you learned to do that? We'll give you a hint: Think outside the box.

---

script as he goes along." And polls around the state suggest that people are feeling the impact of his fresh vision. We are trying very hard not to be Pollyannas in the State of Maine, and Governor King's contribution, in part, is to help us avoid being caught up in the hubris of success.

There's Still Time to Change Your Ways

So far we have tried to enlighten you to the symptoms you might exhibit under the Pollyanna syndrome. We listed six reasons companies fail, all themes we will develop in the chapters that follow. As you begin your personal journey in the pages that follow, we want to emphasize the positive.

If you have made mistakes, celebrate those mistakes because in celebrating them you have to first identify them. And as long as you are willing to recognize the symptoms and act, there is time for you and your company to turn around and enjoy future successes.

During a recent interview, Rory Strunk—the high-tech sports media entrepreneur who is also an early commercial participant on the Internet's World Wide Web—provided us with the perfect summation of what's most important in business: "There are three things in business that I feel are essential: enthusiasm, creativity, and perseverance." Notice that Rory did not say making money, although that is certainly a desirable and needed by-product of the other three components. We want to reinforce his message by encouraging you to build *enthusiasm* for the job ahead, apply your personal brand of *creativity,* and be *persistent* in your task. And, we might add, be proactive not reactive. Take the initiative.

Rory is an example of an entrepreneur who has taken his share of business risks with all the enthusiasm, creativity, and perseverance he could muster. He has positioned his Resort Sports Network (an innovation in its own right) on the Internet and used it to promote dozens of US ski resorts. One way he moved beyond the crowd was to place a television camera on top of several of the mountains. Photos of the ski area and current conditions are downloaded to the World Wide Web at regular intervals. To take a look, visit his Web site at http://www.rsn.com/.

Still think you're not a Pollyanna? Still believe your market share is impenetrable and your successful business will go on forever? Read on. We intend not only to make a believer out of you but also to help you do something before failure is staring you in the face. In the movie version of *Pollyanna,* the town's fire-and-brimstone-spouting preacher warned his congregation: "Death comes unexpectedly." We would add that in business it is sometimes accidentally self-inflicted by a management and employees who fail to realize they have a problem.

Just remember, all the steps we will suggest are simple, almost deceptively so. But they aren't easy; to accomplish them you need to look deep within yourself and your organization. You need to be brutally honest, and then you need to adopt our simple steps as your credo. It must become a process you live and breathe and perform every day.

As you pack your bags for the journey ahead, take three essential concepts with you:

- Observe yourself and the world around you. This will help you keep in touch with the market as well as with your own creativity.
- Remember, past success is no guarantee for future success.
- Develop a fresh perspective—a new way of looking at your business, its problems, and the opportunities around you.

CHAPTER 2

Lulled to Sleep by Success? Wake Up!

"Even if you're on the right track, you'll get run over if you just sit there."
—Will Rogers

Pollyanna Takes a Hit

"Everything yields to success, even grammar," wrote the French novelist Victor Hugo. Unfortunately, it's true. Your vision, your knowledge of the competition, your sense of humility, your edge, and, ultimately, your business all yield to success and the triple threat of arrogance, ignorance, and complacency, which success breeds. So stay alert.

> **Your vision, your knowledge of the competition, your sense of humility, your edge, and, ultimately, your business all yield to success and the triple threat of arrogance, ignorance, and complacency, which success breeds. So stay alert.**

Let's now just suppose the worst—you have fallen victim to great success and have become a full-fledged member of the Loyal Order of Pollyannas. In your isolation and complacency, you've missed all the early warning signals that suggest your business is in trouble, such as employees grumbling among themselves, customers ever so gradually turning to your competition's products, or a new competitor creeping up from some sector of the economy you had never viewed as a threat. It's not surprising you haven't seen the signs. During the early stages, when your business first starts to sour, it continues to move forward for a while on its own momentum. The slowdown can be almost imperceptible. Then suddenly you notice revenues have taken a little hit. Your first inclination may be to assume this is just a blip on the radar screen and things will soon turn around. But they don't; full-scale trouble erupts. What are you going to do? If you are like most Pollyannas, you'll go down one of two paths. You'll either cut costs or cut prices. Both are short-term fixes at best and at worst could kill your company.

> "There is a truism in business that there is no such thing as a one-quarter disappointment. Generally companies really don't know what hit them in the first quarter. It takes them a period of time to straighten it out and get back on track. I have a rule in terms of investing that generally we won't buy a company until it's had four down quarters . . . Then I want to make sure that the business is tracking upward."—Richard Aster

Beware the Hubris Curve

The simple fact is, success can ruin people as well as companies. We spoke with Michael Stolper—the innovative investment consultant, money manager for the wealthy, founder of Stolper and Company (in business since 1975), and publisher of *Mutual Fund Monthly Newsletter*—about a condition born out of success. Although he was speaking specifically about mutual fund portfolio managers (the proclaimed rock stars of their industry) his comments have even broader applicability. "They climb the Hubris Curve. That's the cliché we use for people who used to be decent human beings but have become insufferable and self-absorbed. It's a combination of reaching very high compensation levels and being relatively error-free for long periods of time. They begin to lose the edge of self-examination and self-doubt. The warning signs are obvious because basically it's a personality change."

The Hubris Curve is a natural condition that, Stolper says, we all must guard against. "When I have a tendency to want to superimpose one of my views of the financial world," he admits, "I'm quick to remind myself that my skill is in identifying talent rather than being able to make those specific financial decisions. So I give myself a lecture every day as to my own limitations, because you do form opinions and it's fun to be right. But my job is not to be right; my job is to enrich our clients. When I subordinate the views of the money managers, people who have demonstrably higher skills than I, to my own view of the world, then I'm about to make a mistake."

Don't Chop before You Think

We're not suggesting a company should never cut costs or reevaluate its pricing structure—quite the opposite in fact. Spiraling costs are often a by-product of growth and success. Hugh Farrington found himself in just such a situation. As the CEO of Hannaford Bros. Co., the 100-plus-store, $2.5 billion supermarket and food retailer, Farrington explained to us that the company had grown rapidly in the 1980s, as did the cost structure for running the larger operation. But as long as inflation continued to rise, the higher costs were offset. "Then all of a sudden inflation was zero," he recalls, "and the piper had to be paid. Going back now, with 20/20 hindsight vision, if I had known in 1985 what I know

today, there isn't any way we would have grown the cost structure of this company as quickly."

The relationship between costs and prices is critical and deserves much of your attention—but on a continous, constructive, proactive basis, not as part of some reactive effort by a management desperate to salvage a bad quarter. When management elects cost cutting over reengineering because it fears the latter will be too complicated and take too long, that's a red flag that the proposed cost cutting could be potentially lethal. It probably means the real problems have gone unaddressed.

What makes cost cutting so attractive is its ability almost to guarantee a boost to profits—at least short term—which, if you're public and have to answer to shareholders, can drive you to restrict your actions to the quick fix. As the CEO of another national company lamented to us, "I only wish I did not have to report to my shareholders for two years so I could really do what I think is the most effective job for the company and position it for the years ahead. Unfortunately, we're focused on short-term profits and short-term margins. The way we run our business for the short term is, in fact, detrimental to our long-term success."

Lest we sound otherwise, we believe there is a practical and positive approach to cost cutting. But it demands that intelligence and common sense be applied in liberal doses. For example, General Electric actually fixed problems by consolidating, selling some parts of its business and putting money into other efforts. In the process, the company cut its backlog and turnaround time. Rather than just cut costs when competitors cut costs, GE won market share from competitors without trying to increase overall market share—a much more difficult position to sustain.

Business is not the only venue for common sense as applied to cost cutting. Governor Angus King is cutting costs of state government in Maine. His challenge is to save $155 million while keeping state employee morale high. His approach is to look for real opportunities—reducing duplication of effort, downsizing through reorganization—rather than just cutting indiscriminately across the board, as many politicians have done.

Pollyannas, on the other hand, slash costs in exchange for instant gains to the bottom line. But cost cutting is never as easy as, "We'll cut 10 percent across the board and go from there." The trickle-down effects are staggering. If you resort blindly to taking 10 percent off the top, you may butcher your cash cows. As the saying goes, "Americans think of the next quarter, the Japanese of the next quarter century." Let's evaluate the damage that such a philosophy can cause to your company. When cost cutting is the order of the day, internally, growth plans are reevaluated, research and development is cut, distribution tightens, and morale descends into the subterranean boweis of the company. It isn't long before customers feel the impact. Perhaps a customer who used to push your products decides your cost cutting has reduced the quality of your product. He either drops your line or discourages all but the most persistent customers from buying your products. Or maybe the customer feels your service is just not what it used to be. In either case, another company or another product fills the gap, and presto, you've lost another customer! In the end, cost will be the least of the things you have cut. When you cut costs, you risk cutting profits.

> Or maybe the retailer fears your service is just not what it used to be. In either case, another company or another product fills the gap, and presto, you've lost another customer! In the end, cost will be the least of the things you have cut. When you cut costs, you risk cutting profits.

King Tut Never Planned for Change

World history is littered with Pollyannas who suffered the ill effects of success. Ancient Egypt, for example, enjoyed a stable, orderly, complacent form of government that prevailed for more than 3,000 years. Egyptians were content in their vision of the world, ruled by all-powerful pharaohs and a bevy of immortal gods. At the same time, the Egyptians' complacency and aversion to change did not protect their society from intermittent periods of violent upheaval.

Not unlike the company ravaged by the effects of knee-jerk cost cutting, Egyptian society was disrupted time and again because it lacked a course of steady, progressive change. And because of the very nature of the upheavals, which usually occurred when a weak pharoah sat on the throne or outside forces threatened society, true change was never an outcome. Only disruption. Beware the curse of complacency.

Yet management repeats this fatal error over and over again because it sees only the initial spike in profits. The domino effect we've described is harder for management to trace. So when profits decline again, managers often will respond by cutting some more. This is a going-out-of-business strategy if ever we've seen one.

When you have determined that you really need to cut costs, start with a companywide audit. Identify the programs, products, services, and research that aren't pulling their weight. Determine which ones are least strategic to the business. Then and only then, start to cut.

A variation on our cost-cutting scenario is price cutting. There are times when lowering prices can be a direct result of efficiencies gained from applying new technology or reengineering or reinventing the company. Lowering prices, while lowering costs of production—thus retaining your margin—can be a valuable differentiator in the market. Just don't subscribe to the school of business that believes you can discount prices and make up the difference in volume. All that does is put you out of business twice as fast.

The airline industry offers a good example of reactive price cutting. Back in the 50s and 60s, we chose our airlines based on our destination. Pan Am and TWA, for example, were the primary American carriers to Europe. Delta and Eastern took us to Florida. American, United, and TWA were the nonstop choices to California. In addition, there were

It's in Their Blood

It's been said that successful entrepreneurs who are drawn from other industries into the airline business suffer for having "jet fuel in their veins." Howard Hughes, Eddie Rickenbacher, Carl Ichan, and Freddy Laker are all examples, and now Richard Branson. The irreverent English entrepreneur first built a successful record empire, Virgin Records, which he sold to fund his venture into the skies. So far, Virgin Air has limited routes—primarily between New York and London, and Boston and London. But Branson has built some special amenities into his offering—limousine service, preflight meal vouchers, in-flight massages—and still kept the price reasonable. British Air, feeling Virgin Air's presence in the marketplace, used the courts to try to curtail its business and ultimately its chances of survival. Branson won round one. What's next? Will the sky be his limit? Can he continue to deliver what the customer wants? What will happen should he decide to put 50 jets into service? If he tries to compete on price, he may find his pockets aren't deep enough. Stay tuned.

many smaller, regional airlines. When airlines were deregulated in the late 1970s, the carriers were free to compete for routes into any airport where they could get gate space. Delta, for example, one of the major carriers along the Eastern corridor, started flying not only coast-to-coast but also to Europe. Everyone wanted the lucrative routes: New York to Chicago to California and New York to London to the rest of Europe.

As a result, air travel became a commodity. All the major carriers began competing with one another for the same customer base, and the only way to significantly increase the size of the customer base—the number of people flying—was to lower fares. But if one carrier dropped prices on a particular route or offered a special fare, the others quickly followed suit. More people were flying, but many at deep discounts. And the customer today is sophisticated enough to shop for the lowest fare.

In an attempt to preserve customer loyalty, the airlines turned to frequent-flyer programs as a way to encourage customers to always fly their airline. In recent years, the airlines have given away hundreds of thousands of free flights, enough so that now airlines are reevaluating and restructuring these programs. Today, many of the major carriers actually are losing money, and a few have gone out of business. While the airlines' problems can't all be attributed to price cutting, its impact is undisputed.

The plight of the airlines is almost an instant replay of the Virginia tobacco farmers' saga in the late 17th and early 18th centuries. In 1618, colonists hit upon a cash crop—tobacco. Although this was only one of many crops that grew well in the warm, damp climate of Virginia, it was the only one as good as money. One could get rich growing tobacco, so naturally everyone wanted to grow it. But the increased volume—with every planter competing for the same market—soon drove down the price, and in the end only a few tobacco farmers made money. In less than a hundred years, many of the great plantation families were deep in debt. The airline business now faces the challenge of trying to rewrite this lesson in history.

While we're on the subject, let's consider the problems of the retail sector during the past couple of years—a condition, we might add, retailers have brought on themselves in large part. In an effort to attract customers, they have staged one sale after another. In their efforts to boost end-of-the-year figures, they have supplanted the post-Christmas sales with pre-Christmas sales. And savvy consumers have sat back, biding their time, waiting for the inevitable 25 percent to 30 percent discount, available just in time for last-minute holiday shopping. It appears retailers will have their job cut out for them in turning around this trend.

However, in cost-cutting, as in anything else, there are exceptions to every rule. There will always be severe cases where management has had to stop the boat from leaking before it could set a course and start planning proactively. Jim Shaffer is president and CEO of Guy Gannett Communications in Portland, Maine, and a newspaperman at heart with more than 25 years in the business—including senior management positions with the *Los Angeles Times* and the *Sun-Times* company. During a recent interview, Shaffer shared such an experience, and told us how even the classic turnaround can include long-term planning:

"It's a great compliment that you call me visionary now. But in 1991, I was the finger-pointing autocrat. In June 1991, when I was brought into the company, it was unprofitable, with rising debt and a bank default looming. I was brought in as a turnaround executive. I was supposed to fix the things that turnaround executives are supposed to fix. We sold the radio division, which was cash negative. We shut down papers in Minnesota that were cash negative. We combined plants in Minnesota. We combined plants in Maine. We are talking about major strategic moves executed rapidly. We had to; there was an urgent situation. When the building is burning, you don't talk about the philosophy of architecture. It was autocratic almost . . . recruit, fix, sell, largely dictated by me. I had been in these situations before; I knew what had to be done, and time was of the essence. The focus was on individual performance, mostly mine and some key executives'.

"By '92, it was clear that we did have a turnaround in the works, so we started shifting our strategy and our whole thinking about strategy. During the phase we labeled *strategizing,* we moved into management development, and a more granular level of cost controls started to emerge. Revenue development became more important. Prior to this, the problems weren't very complicated and not in need of visualization. They were urgent but not complicated.

"A University of Michigan professor I know defines success as when the problems get more complicated. Well, the problems are starting to get more complicated now, so new skills are needed to deal with them. Hence, we are creating an organization for innovation, adaptivity, human resource strategy and execution, empowerment, and leadership.

"With the fires out, I had a chance to do some reading and thinking and study high-performance organizations elsewhere. There are some in the media business, but most are outside. Common characteristics of the organizations were committed, empowered employees and a balance of authority where top management didn't just dictate everything from the top."

In the end, the tactics you choose should reflect the big picture— your vision for the company and your strategy for achieving that goal. At the end of the day you need to *manage* costs, but don't cut costs just to stimulate profits. Rather, examine your business first and find out why profits are down, then make the necessary changes.

Look for the Cracks

One of the themes we repeat throughout this book is the need to be proactive. *Reactive behavior is the sole domain of Pollyanna.* Unfortunately, it requires a lot more effort to be proactive than to be reactive. As Italian political theorist Niccolò Machiavelli wrote almost 500 years ago in *The Prince*: "There is nothing more difficult to take in hand, more perilous to conduct, or more uncertain in its success, than to take the lead in the introduction of a new order of things." Despite his reputation as a reactionary, Machiavelli did have insight.

All too often, it appears easier to focus on bringing down the competition than on creating a unique competitive advantage—a niche of

Crash-Test Your Business

Pilots prepare for disaster by running their worst-case scenarios on a flight simulator. Engine failure, wind shears, broken landing gear, severe storms—anything goes, and the pilots try to develop a course of action that will get them through each situation without mishap. Companies can practice much the same thing, and they don't need a million-dollar computer to do it.

Phase 1: Start by gathering all your staff and brainstorming some of the possible scenarios the business could face over the next couple of years: unexpected competition, demand for products outstripping your ability to produce, economic recession, introduction of new technology that makes your product or service obsolete. Try to develop scenarios that anticipate both the growth and the decline of the business.

Try to develop scenarios that anticipate both the growth and the decline of the business.

Phase 2: Take your list and reverse-engineer each scenario. Think about how you would handle rapid growth or survive a massive change in your industry. What is the worst thing that could happen in each case? In other words, stress test your company's ability to act. This is not unlike the exercise public companies use when planning a defense, such as a poison pill, to counter a possible takeover attempt. You are just extending the scenarios to anticipate a wider range of business situations.

Think of this exercise as a fire-drill for your company.

---

one's own. Today, for example, many software entrepreneurs are spending their time and energy crying that Bill Gates and his band of merry followers in Redmond, Washington, are making it harder for them to get their piece of the high-tech market. Just as all guns used to be aimed on IBM, today Microsoft is the target. Much of Gates's competition is eager to have the Justice Department play the role of Saint George and smite the mighty software dragon, or at least cut him down to size.

With the introduction of Windows 95, the complaints have focused on a possible unfair advantage Microsoft may have in bundling the access software to its on-line network with the operating system. It's just too easy to hook up, grumble the other on-line services, which distribute their free disks by polybagging them with various computer and lifestyle magazines.

Perhaps. But there is no denying that Gates has been delivering what customers want. Rather than plotting Microsoft's demise, the budding Pollyannas in high tech should be looking for opportunities where they can establish a niche of their own and build from there. They should be looking ahead and asking themselves where the next innovation will come from. The Internet? Television? Telephone companies? Or some combination of all the above?

In fact, Microsoft's competitors would do well to focus on the advantages and opportunities the software giant offers: First, with all the advance hype that accompanies a major new release, companies have time—often a couple of years—to prepare a course of action. Second, it's impossible for Microsoft to offer everything to everyone. There are many opportunities for business. Companies just need to plan strategically what they can provide and market better than Microsoft can. Third, Microsoft is bound to create enormous sales for its primary products. This will create opportunities for after-market sales, such as utilities and enhancements.

> **Rather than plotting Microsoft's demise, the budding Pollyannas in high tech should be looking for opportunities where they can establish a niche of their own and build from there.**

As entrepreneurs, you need to keep one eye on the competition and the other scanning the marketplace for new opportunities. For example, Kimberly-Clark's Kleenex is an icon among brand names and much better known than Microsoft among the population at large. It's hard to imagine anyone competing against it, yet a number of companies do. Take, for example, Procter & Gamble's Puffs facial tissues, which positions itself as softer and easier on the nose. P&G has focused on a value-added feature that effectively distinguishes Puffs from Kleenex.

You need to be proactive in finding the opportunities that will not only help you survive but enable you to grow as well. Often you'll find your opportunity in a niche—a crack or seam the competition has overlooked. Picture three spheres of influence—marketplace, media, and customer—and apply their response to a new offering to your product or service. Ask yourself, for example, What is the media covering? Perhaps computers and software. What are customers thinking? Are they saying, "I've got to have that"? What's happening in the marketplace? Is there a lot of media hype, is there a learning curve? Has the industry redefined

If you still have doubts about the Pollyanna syndrome, take note of this recent article from *The Wall Street Journal:*

Apple of America's Eye Falls Victim to Pride

If Apple Computer—now in takeover talks—ceases to be an independent company, it will be far more than an ordinary business story. For Apple has never been an ordinary company, and its key product, the Macintosh computer, isn't just another machine. More than any other single organization, private or public, Apple is responsible for making technology cool and approachable, ushering in the era of the personal computer that is now transforming the world faster than we can chronicle the change. Its apparent failure to survive as an independent business, largely due to self-inflicted wounds, is an object lesson that great products and bold visions alone can't produce corporate success.

Indeed, in the history of postwar American capitalism, it's hard to think of a product with more influence, and a more fanatical customer following, than the Macintosh computer—or of one that was hobbled by as many bad management decisions on the part of its maker.

In its 19-year history, Apple has become the stuff of legend, literally starting up in a garage, and eventually becoming an $11 billion company—still nearly twice as large as Microsoft but far less profitable. More important, in that short time, Apple pulled off two great changes in the way people think about and use technology—"paradigm shifts," as Apple founder Steve Jobs liked to call them. One was to popularize the personal computer itself, and the other was to establish the best way to make it usable by non-technical people—the Macintosh way, with a mouse and a "graphical user interface" of icons and menus instead of complex commands.

In the process, Apple forced every other computer company, including bitter rivals like IBM and Microsoft, to follow its lead. And it established its brand name and the familiar rainbow-colored Apple logo as among the best-known, and most positively regarded, in the world.

What's more, Apple's entrepreneurial rise from rags to riches became a sort of American business fable, cited in countless books, articles and speeches as proof of the rightness of the American system. U.S. presidents liked to associate themselves with the story, right up through Bill Clinton, who wooed the company politically and seated Apple CEO John Sculley next to Mrs. Clinton at his first State of the Union address.

But while Apple won the war for computing, it lost the battle of the marketplace to companies like Microsoft, whose product ideas were far less bold but whose business skills were far better.

The first of Apple's two great feats, which Mr. Jobs performed in 1977 with his co-founder Stephen Wozniak, was the Apple II computer. It was the first PC to really penetrate the public consciousness, the first to be widely used in business and education. When IBM assembled its team to build its own first PC years later, it reportedly used Apple IIs to help manage the project, despite Big Blue's public dismissal of the little machine. Even now, long after Apple stopped making them, Apple IIs are churning away in thousands of schools.

Apple's next and greatest stroke came in 1984 with the Mac, which applied pioneering work done in the labs of Xerox to a commercially viable personal computer. At its debut in 1984, the machine was underpowered and widely mocked. Few "serious" computer jockeys would even use it. But gradually, the "computer for the rest of us" developed a formidable following.

Not only was the Mac's interface far easier to use, but over the years it distinguished itself from IBM clones by coming complete with sound, good video, networking and many other capabilities that became standard only years later on competing machines. Setting up a Mac was a piece of cake compared with the technical torture required to get an IBM clone going.

Soon, the Mac became a cult object. Using brilliant marketing, and its own corporate fable, Apple wove a sort of cool, counterculture aura around the Mac, making it the favorite tool of opinion makers in journalism, Hollywood, universities and the arts. It hired "evangelists" to persuade software companies to make Mac products. And its first Mac TV ad, portraying IBM as a dictatorial Big Brother being smashed by Apple, remains one of the most famous commercials ever.

But the very success of the cult of the Mac planted the seeds of Apple's business demise. The company began to believe its own PR. Even after Mr. Jobs was replaced by Mr. Sculley, a former Pepsi marketer, Apple often lacked a coherent business plan. It functioned in many ways more as a church than a corporation, certain that its followers and their Macs would inherit the earth, without sweating the details of how. The company saw no need until too late to stop charging a high premium for its machines. It eventually began stiffing software developers. Worse, Apple contemptuously underestimated competitors—especially the relentless chief of Microsoft, Bill Gates, who worked for years to bring the Mac's approach to the more numerous IBM compatibles.

Blinded by arrogance, Apple and Mr. Sculley blew it big in the late 1980s, when they passed up a chance to license the Mac's popular operating system to other computer makers to permit Mac clones. That was just before Mr. Gates finally managed to bring out a truly useful version of his Macintosh-imitating software for IBM compatibles, called Windows. If Apple's decision had gone otherwise, it's doubtful Microsoft would be ruling the computer business today, or that Mr. Gates would be America's richest man.

That huge blunder was compounded by another. The company let its famous operating system go without a major rewrite for years, standing still so long that Mr. Gates was finally able to match the Mac's key software features in Windows 95 last year. Meanwhile, IBM and other computer makers started building into their machines most of the Mac's hardware features and simplifying the setup process.

There were other big mistakes. Apple first commercialized the laser printer, but lost the bulk of the market to Hewlett-Packard when it failed to make versions of the printers that could work with non-Apple computers. It squandered a big lead in notebook computers by failing to revise its popular PowerBook line fast enough. The company even blew the Internet. Years ago, Apple actually popularized a simple programming language for creating hyper-linked documents, the same concept that a new upstart, Netscape, is exploiting to transform the Internet's World Wide Web into a huge business opportunity. But Apple let its hypertext product, HyperCard, wither on the vine.

Apple's last great effort at a third paradigm shift, the Newton handheld computer, bombed when Mr. Sculley over-promised its planned ability to understand handwriting. In recent months, the company has been developing a machine called Pippin that could become the kind of cheap "information appliance" that will likely succeed the PC in many homes in coming years. But Apple's top brass, under stolid and unimaginative CEO Michael Spindler, hasn't made any move to rush the machine to market as an Apple product, instead merely licensing it to a game company in Japan.

So it looks as though Apple may be independent no more, and we'll all be a little poorer for it, even those who never owned a Mac. None of the other big computer companies, including Microsoft, seems ready to take Apple's place as the source of big innovations. But the laws of the marketplace bring down those who ignore them, no matter how cool they think they are.

Walter S. Mossberg, "Apple of America's Eye Falls Victim to Pride," *The Wall Street Journal*, January 24, 1996, Section B, p. 1.

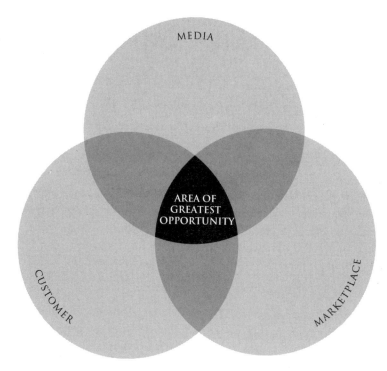

Marketplace Media Customer

itself to meet the new wave? Where the answers to these questions overlap is where you will find opportunity.

Here's another example of how to look for the cracks: With the advent of technological and process breakthroughs that have created manufacturing and distribution revolutions (such as just-in-time inventory) and megasuccesses (such as Federal Express), the logistics industry is one that many an eager entrepreneur should be evaluating for potential. According to a 1995 *The Wall Street Journal* article by Jon Bigness, contract logistic services are expected to triple over the next five years, with a projected annual revenue topping $50 billion.*

The media are all astir with articles about outsourcing and the global market for services. Customers are eager to find qualified services

---

*Jon Bigness, "Driving Force," *The Wall Street Journal,* September 6, 1995, Section A; p. 1,
    Column 6.

that can meet their needs. The marketplace is open to global competition. It will be difficult to separate the wheat from the chaff when trying to select the service providers who can meet the challenge.

Perhaps the industry could benefit from a service that helps match customers with vendors. Perhaps it helps to evaluate the quality of work performed. Maybe that service could take the form of a highly specialized industry newsletter or a more broadly circulated magazine. Since we know certain magazines already serve this industry, the first order of the day would be to study circulation rates. Have they grown in relation to market activity? If not, why not? If so, is there a smaller but growing branch of the logistics industry that deserves better coverage? Or maybe the industry needs an independent evaluation service that cannot be swayed by advertising dollars? Thus entrepreneurs examine and evaluate the potential of a new niche.

It's amazing how simple a niche sometimes can be. Scott Cook of Intuit Software, Howard Schultz of Starbucks, and Scott Beck of Boston Market all found their "crack" in convenience. These entrepreneurs have enjoyed great success by meeting our needs in the 90s for services and products designed to make our lives easier. In a time when we are forever rushing around and feeling inconvenienced, Intuit software has simplified our home and small-business accounting. Starbucks has made it easy and pleasurable for us to relax briefly over a cup of gourmet coffee. And Boston Market gives us "a just like homemade" taste at the speed and prices of a fast-food restaurant.

Identifying your niche is more than just an exercise. It can (1) open up growth opportunities for your business, (2) provide you with an added value that enables you to compete with companies many times your size, and (3) allow you to find and build upon the things that differentiate you from your competition.

In identifying your niche, you need to be realistic about its potential for success. Therefore, we recommend measuring your ideas against the following criteria:

1. *Standard.* If a 3 percent error, let's say, is the industry standard, yours must be 3 percent or better.

2. *Need.* You have to identify a niche that reflects what customers want. You can test need by applying the three converging spheres of influence (marketplace, media, customer).

3. *Latent need.* If you have a radically new concept or technology, you may not find customers just waiting for you to go to market. They often don't understand why they will need your product. Fax

machines, modems, beepers, and bottled water are all successful products that started as latent needs. You must build need by educating prospective customers as to the benefits of your product or service.

Although the concept of establishing a niche is simple, the effort will require hard work, creativity, an open mind, and a clear understanding of your market and industry. To understand niche markets better, let's see how still other companies have defined their niche.

> **Although the concept of establishing a niche is simple, the effort will require hard work, creativity, an open mind, and a clear understanding of your market and industry.**

There's a small fast-food restaurant called Rapid Ray's on Main Street in Saco, Maine. It sells the usual fare—hamburgers and hot dogs—and there is no place to sit down. Yet it does a thriving business down the street from McDonald's, Burger King, and a variety of other national food chains. Why? Great food, combined with fast, efficient service. And Rapid Ray's has a personal touch that appeals to the locals: The employees remember your name and speak to you as a friend when you come in.

Service may be the most important, and possibly the most overlooked, niche. It is certainly the most obvious one for small businesses to use when competing against discount houses and chains. You seldom can beat large companies on price—at least not and stay in business—but you almost always (some say 8 times out of 10) can beat them on service. Remember, even though we all take advantage of low prices, most of us are predisposed to want to trade with a local company, a friend, or a neighbor, especially one who can give us an added value we can't find elsewhere. A certain pet store in Portland, Maine, is very popular and competes well against the discount pet chains. The owner remembers his customers—both the four-legged and two-legged variety—and even sends birthday cards to the animals.

There's a car dealer in rural Maine. He's located about 75 miles from Portland, but not only can he get you the car you want, he beats everyone else in town on price because his overhead is low. He also services the car and makes the task easier than going to a local mechanic. A driver comes down early in the morning, brings you a loaner car, takes your car back, then returns your car the next morning. The dealer's niche is both price and service.

In the 1970s, Theodore Levitt wrote that everything can be differentiated. To make service your niche, you have to exceed expectations. By exceeding expectations, you are adding value. Service, for example, is being able to get a refrigerator to someone's home within two hours of the purchase, when the larger stores require two to five days for delivery.

But service is not the only niche available. Michael Ruettgers is a good example of a CEO who recognizes the power of information, both as an increasingly valuable commodity today and in the future and as a market niche. His company, EMC Corporation, which made its debut on the Fortune 500 list in 1993, offers an alternative to corporations that need more computer storage and faster systems as their own demands for information increase. In the past, meeting a company's growing demands for information processing meant replacing its current mainframe with a larger and faster model. Now, however, in many cases EMC's storage devices can do the job for a fraction of the cost of a new mainframe.

Ruettgers also realizes that the information technology industry continues to change quickly. He is using that knowledge to keep his company poised on the crest of industry developments. As companies increasingly move to adopt distributed computing solutions, EMC is expanding its product line to include storage devices for network systems.

Idexx, a firm in Westbrook, Maine, has found a profit center niche in the research-intensive biotech industry. Rather than follow suit with other biotech firms and spend all its money and effort on research, Idexx has taken a different tack. To create new products, Idexx often licenses the breakthrough work of other companies. And it is turning a profit in the process, a feat that still eludes many in the biotech business. For example, Idexx uses the research of others, combined with its own small (50-person) R&D staff, to create diagnostic tests for use by veterinarians. It has created successful heartworm and Lyme disease tests for dogs, feline leukemia tests, and several tests for the poultry and cattle industry.

As you'll discover, many companies fail to find their rightful niche on their first try. Still others have missed the boat completely.

Levi Strauss had the durable clothing business all sewn up. But realizing a drop in jean sales, Levi's tried to broaden its niche by moving into dress clothing. It was the wrong move, and it took Levi's a while to understand that customers who saw it as the premier work-clothes company did not want to buy Levi's dress clothing. The company failed to accurately assess its three spheres of influence. It retrenched but did not give up. The second time, Levi's got it right. Dockers—the new label on neat, trim, casual clothing that's as comfortable as an old pair of jeans— represents the ideal opportunity.

In the last 10 years or so, many companies have used environmental concerns to create a niche. They herald their products as "green" and "eco-friendly." But, as some have discovered, calling products biodegradable because they will disintegrate in a landfill—sooner or later—can backfire as people become more sophisticated about what it really means to be environmentally conscious.

Norway, on the other hand, did it right. The Norwegians wanted to apply environmental awareness and action to the 1994 Winter Olympics effort. On a large scale, this influenced the design and development of the various sports venues. But the Norwegians applied the same princi- ples even to the smallest details—including disposable plates. In calcu- lating the enormous amount of trash the Olympics would create for Lille- hammer, officials opted for a unique solution: the potato plate, a plate made of potato starch that can dissolve in water or be fed to the pigs.

Sometimes when a large company starts losing market share to smaller companies within a hot niche, it tries to move in and take over. Sometimes the large company succeeds, but often it falls on its face try- ing. For example, the beer industry has lost ground to the proliferation of more than 200 microbreweries in the United States. The big brewers tried to regain their market share by creating their own pseudo-microbrewery brands. But they were caught at their own game by a public that hates being tricked. A second effort, somewhat more successful, has been for the large breweries to buy out some of the popular microbreweries. This strategy can work—and work well for both companies—provided the parent company allows the entrepreneurial venture to keep its indepen- dence and culture as a separate subsidiary.

How to manage a wholly owned subsidiary that has an established niche is precisely the issue before General Motors with its Saturn brand today. In 1985, a high-powered committee at GM decided the only way out of the company's doldrums was to create a new car division, the first for GM since Chevrolet was created in 1917. Then-chairman Roger B. Smith called it an opportunity to start fresh. The cost to GM was $5 billion.

Since the first car rolled off the assembly line in 1990, Saturn has enjoyed good press, in part due to some smart public relations work, and in June 1995 Saturn ranked number one in the sales satisfaction index as calculated by independent evaluators J. D. Power and Associates. The Sat-

The Butterfly Effect

Size can be an effective niche and open great opportunities, as it has for the Chileans, who are succeeding in their efforts to break into the Japanese market. As Roberto de Andraca, chairman of Cap Industries, one of the five largest companies in Chile, explained, when an American company comes in, it brings part of the United States with it. It's big, like an elephant. When it comes through the door, it knocks the door off its hinges. Your natural instinct is to be defensive and stop the elephant.

Chile, de Andraca continued, is small, like a butterfly. A butterfly can go under the door. It doesn't have to knock it down. You're better off being a butterfly than an elephant if you want to operate in different markets today.

Small companies can fly under the radar, so to speak. This is to your competitive advantage. So put it to work. The 3M company has tried to apply this principle by breaking the company apart internally. The internal division helps 3M maintain its entrepreneurial approach without abandoning the whole business. It allows divisions to think and act like butterflies, yet gives them the support of the whole company. Large companies need to slow their forward momentum before they can even start to move in a new direction. Smaller companies and smaller units of large companies have greater agility. In a sense this was what enabled IBM's PC to get started; the PC division acted like a separate company, down in Boca Raton, Florida, out of sight of headquarters.

urn initiative is now 10 years old, and company officials report that Saturn has enjoyed an operating profit since 1993. On the other hand, the division has hardly made a dent in paying back the $5 billion in start-up money. Now GM is looking at the niche that was supposed to help reestablish GM, trying to decide whether or not the company should bring Saturn back into the fold in order to increase productivity and whether Saturn technology and processes can be transferred to other GM sites.

In recent years, Hollywood seems to have adopted a different approach to niche marketing, one we'll call the "me-too" niche. Whatever the most recent box office hit, Hollywood follows with sequels and knock-offs as quickly as possible. In the 1980s the success of *Rambo* and *The Terminator* elicited a string of violent action films. More recently it's been the sweep of kick-boxing movies. And once actor Jim Carrey revived the dumb and dumber theme, many others have tried to cash in. Hollywood rides a trend into the ground, then jumps on the next one. But beware: This strategy won't work for everyone. Copycats seldom beat the original. It's always better to find your own unique angle, if not your own niche.

On the other hand, the United Society of Believers in Christ's Second Appearing, better known as the Shakers, never did cash in on their niche. Beyond being a religious sect, the Shakers had a business niche in the beautifully understated simplicity and complete practicality of the furniture and household products they made. But they made everything by hand, which prevented them from competing in a mechanized and automated world. Other companies came along and applied Shaker principles and designs to modern manufacturing techniques and beat the Shakers both on price and on the volume of product they could deliver. As a result, Shaker designs have outlasted their creators, who are all but extinct.

> **Copycats seldom beat the original. It's always better to find your own unique angle, if not your own niche.**

The Shakers are far from alone in this category of failed niche makers. Oceangoing shipbuilders in the United States have followed suit. For years they could navigate the halls of Congress to win large, lucrative naval contracts, and their ability to supply U.S. defense needs in World War II is legendary. But as contracts and need have dried up, these shipbuilders have failed to reposition themselves to compete for a piece of the international merchant shipbuilding market. Today, therefore, Japan leads the world in merchant shipbuilding. In 1993, Japan had 31 percent of the market, with South Korea in second place with 20 percent. The United States held 27th place with a paltry 0.2 percent of the merchant shipbuilding market.

Before we conclude this discussion of the niche, let's look at the cases of the Walt Disney Company and Wang Laboratories. Both developed successful niches. Both enjoyed the kind of success that lulled them to sleep. Both have struggled to break out of their Pollyanna straitjackets. Their success is another story.

We shouldn't be surprised that the Walt Disney Company found itself lulled to sleep by years of success. Almost from the day in 1928 when Walt Disney released *Steamboat Willie*, the first animated cartoon with sound, the company was a success. From cartoons, Disney

Play 20/20 Hindsight

We all have the power of 20/20 hindsight. We use it to second-guess the quarterback on Monday morning or to play "if only I knew then what I know now." But these are fruitless activities. There is, however, one constructive use for your 20/20 hindsight. Look for companies that have stood at the fork in the road and had to make a decision. Then assess their choices. Did they see their niche? Or did they miss a bigger opportunity? Here's one to get you started:

Apple co-founder Steven Jobs recognized the commercial and technological value of the interactive graphical user interface (GUI) when he saw the work being done at Xerox's Palo Alto Research Center. Jobs had the vision to apply Xerox's invention—an ability that has eluded Xerox more than once over the years—but was he too blinded by his dedication to the Macintosh to see the larger market for GUI? Did he miss the ultimate niche by not moving beyond his own hardware platform and creating a world of computers operating under his interface? In other words, could Windows have been an Apple product?

The intent of this exercise is to get you to focus on the power of a niche to make or break a company. You'll find, too, the more you study other companies' niches, the better you'll become at identifying your own.

---

graduated to feature-length animated films that set the standard for the film industry. By the mid-50s, the Disney studios were the premier producers of family movies; the Mickey Mouse Club television show had captured the imagination of a generation of children; and Disney had opened the gates to his crown jewel, Disneyland, in Anaheim, California.

Walt Disney was a rare entrepreneur in that he seems never to have lost sight of his vision and always remained one step ahead of the competition. But Disney died in 1966, and it's hard to say if he could have sustained his vision had he lived another 10 or 15 years. Could he, for example, have adapted his vision for the company to accommodate changes in the American family?

In the early 70s, the Walt Disney Company had reason for concern: The new Orlando, Florida, theme park was off to a slow start. Disney movies didn't pack 'em in like they used to. The Disney morality was out of touch with American youth. Even with all their high-priced special effects, movies like *Tron* and *The Black Cauldron* failed. On top of all this, Mickey and Donald faced new competition from the Muppets and Snoopy.

The Walt Disney Company fought an uphill battle for several years as it struggled to get with the times, build new bridges to its customers, understand the competition in its many forms—television, Hollywood, theme parks—and, most important, identify new opportunities. The turnaround took almost a decade. One of the turning points was the creation of Touchstone Studios, which produces films for more mature audiences.

The Disney Channel, a fledgling when Chairman and CEO Michael D. Eisner arrived, is now a successful cable channel with more than 10 million viewers. Perhaps most important, under Eisner and Roy Disney, nephew of Walt, the feature animation films have regained their box-office power. Starting with *Beauty and the Beast* in 1991, Disney has had a chain of blockbusters not only at the movie theaters but in video sales and related merchandising. The Walt Disney Company has almost doubled its revenues since 1990, surpassing the $10 billion mark in 1994.

The cornerstone of the new Disney niche has been to create first-class content: syndicated programming, movies, software, magazines, books, theme parks, resorts, cable programming, cartoons, and an athletic team. As it has played out, this content has enabled Disney to get access to all the distribution it needs. And now the company has that too. The $19 billion acquisition of Capital Cities/ABC virtually completed the picture.

Wang is another story all together. In its early days, Wang Laboratories, too, was led by a visionary—Dr. An Wang—who created a computer empire. He started the company in 1951 with $600. He first scored big with calculators, and over the years he introduced several innovations in the typesetting business with new digital electronic devices. He then revolutionized word processing with dedicated word-processing workstations.

An Wang knew what the customer wanted and dominated the midsize computer market for several years. The company peaked in 1988, after almost eight profitable years, with double-digit growth, $3 billion in sales, and 32,000 employees. It became the darling of the Boston Beltway with buildings scattered all along Route 128.

As Dr. Wang acknowledged in his autobiography, *Lessons:* "Markets change, tastes change, so the companies and the individuals who choose to compete in those markets change."* Within just two years,

_____
*Dr. An Wang, *Lessons: An Autobiography* (Reading, MA: Addison-Wesley, 1986), p. 227.

however, Dr. Wang appeared to fall victim to the Pollyanna syndrome. He hadn't continued to watch, or at least appreciate, the changing trends. It seems he didn't understand what the market wanted and therefore failed to deliver. As we see it, Dr. Wang made two fatal errors: First he remained wedded to the high margin he had in his proprietary systems and never stopped hoping he could use his innovative software to beat IBM. As the world moved gradually toward open systems, Wang continued to use proprietary software to sell his hardware. His second mistake was to overlook the significance of the personal computer revolution until 1983—three years after IBM had introduced its PC. Wang Laboratories finally went Chapter 11 in August 1994. Mired in bankruptcy, Wang Laboratories' $60 million headquarters in Lowell, Massachusetts, sold at auction for a mere $525,000.

In case you think Wang was really only a second-tier player, we'll share a personal story that epitomizes the opportunity Wang lost by missing its niche. A division manager in another company explains: "In 1985, I was with a company that put in a new Wang system designed for 50 people. It was a state-of-the-art system at the time, the most modern computer you could buy. On each desk sat a computer terminal connected to the mainframe, which was down the hall in a temperature-controlled room. The monitor featured green text on a black background, which was supposed to be easier on the eyes. That monitor was attached to a flexible, retractable, ultraergonomic arm allowing the user to move it to a comfortable position. All our programs, files, and documents were stored on the mainframe. We didn't use floppy disks. We gained access to the parts of the system we were authorized to enter via a password. When the system was installed, we all had to be trained because we needed to know some elementary coding to perform various operations like word processing and accounting.

"Then one day, someone walked into the office carrying a 128K Macintosh computer. It didn't have any of the computing power we had with the Wang. But the thought that we could carry a self-contained computer that was almost cute, was so compelling. The Mac, as it was called for short, personified the personal-computer revolution: It's all in this little box, and I'm all yours. When you turned it on, the first thing to appear was a smiling face. The Wang had never smiled. It didn't so much as grunt.

"As the 1984 Macintosh ad during the Super Bowl had emphasized, there was no need to be attached to some monolithic brain. We could control our individual computing destiny. And operating it seemed so intuitive. You want to do something? You click on the picture, called an icon, or drag a file across the screen.

"At that point, arguments broke out in the office over who got to use the Macintosh. But calmer minds prevailed, and we simply bought a few more Macs. As that happened, people began taking the Wang out of their office and replacing it with a Macintosh. What happened in this company was happening in businesses, particularly creative businesses, throughout the country. We were so in love with the Macintosh, we'd actually put it in a big bag and lug it home for the weekend."

Could Wang have become the Apple of the 1980s? Maybe not. Did it fall short of its potential? Definitely. And it lacked IBM's strong entrenchment in corporate computing departments to weather a false step this monumental. Today Wang Laboratories is struggling back from bankruptcy as it creates a new niche for itself in the fields of document imaging and workflow technology. Strategic alliances with Unisys and Microsoft and the acquisition of Sigma Imaging and Groupe Bull may give Wang a second chance. At least CEO Joseph M. Tucci recognizes the magnitude of the effort required. In a 1993 interview with *Fortune* magazine, he said, "We need to change by revolution, not evolution."*

Are You Poised for Growth?

As important as creating a niche is, you also need to develop a tough-minded approach to your business. For this topic, we interviewed Richard Aster, the portfolio manager in charge of the top-performing Meridian Fund, and the man investment adviser Michael Stolper identifies as "incurably responsible." Says Stolper, "I could give all my money to Aster and leave the country for 20 years and know that it would be OK." Aster shared with us his strategy for assessing the potential for a small company to grow. It's one you can apply to yourself.

"There are four things we look for in companies," he says, "and I think looking back historically, all successful companies have had them: One is you have to approach a market that's conducive to growth. In other words, if you're looking for growth stocks there's not much sense beating around in the auto industry or the forest products industry. You're going to find growth stocks either in emerging markets or . . . in large

---

*Andrew E. Serwer, "Wang Laboratories; Can This Company Be Saved?" *Fortune,* April 19, 1993, p. 86.

markets where small companies can take a share [niche], like in the retail industry and so forth. To be in a growth area, you've got to have the wind at your back.

"Second, companies need to have an important market share. You can define that in a lot of different ways. You can be a regional banker or retailer who's not big in the whole country, but you have to have an important market share in that region. There are lots of advantages to market share, whether it's efficiencies of production, marketing clout, buying power, access to the financial markets to get better terms, and so forth. Generally the best companies dominate their markets. Usually this means they're a low-cost producer. You will find when the going gets tough, the people with small market share don't do very well and a lot of times disappear.

"The third thing is the financial characteristics of the business. If you're going to be a growth company, you really do have to have the financial characteristics that support the growth. You need a return on equity that will support a growth rate. For example, if you find a company that's growing at the rate of 20 percent or 30 percent, but has a 9 percent or 10 percent return on equity, the growth rate won't hold. It won't work. You can borrow for a while or raise some equity, but if the characteristics of the business aren't there, they're not a good bet for the future. So if we find those kinds of companies that seem to have a nice growth potential but don't have financial characteristics, we get suspicious.

"The final thing is management. You will find, looking back, that all good companies are well managed. Now judging good management is a difficult proposition. It's certainly qualitative; it's not quantitative. And when you go out and visit a company, you can make a judgment. You can check it out. But you're not going to know for sure whether these people are going to be successful or not over a period of time . . . Initially you like to think these people have leadership qualities and motivational skills, especially if they're building all their bases, not just sales. In other words, they're bringing in middle management and top-level management people to support them. They're putting in systems, the controls and so forth. They're building their financial base, which will enable them to grow successfully for a number of years. Then you have to track and see if they do this. It's one thing to run a $100 million company. It's another to run a $500 million, and it's another still to run a $1 billion company. So you just have to track it through and see if they continue to make the right decisions."

We said above that you have to be tough minded about your business, but you also probably need a certain degree of passion. That's the word renowned investment adviser Michael Stolper uses to describe the personality of the ideal portfolio manager. As he puts it, "First and foremost, passion. I have to believe that they [portfolio managers] would be doing this for considerably less money." We think this is a litmus test equally applicable to anyone who owns, runs, or, ideally, is employed in a business.

> We said above that you have to be tough minded about your business, but you also probably need a certain degree of passion.

The second aspect of the portfolio manager personality Stolper goes on to describe, you may think, wavers on obsessiveness: "Second of all, you're looking for patterns of inferential thinking that are grossly overdeveloped. Most people who are good at this business are very one dimensional. If they go to the grocery store, they are curious as to which products have gotten more shelf space. They are interested in pricing, and they see everything through the prism of a possible investment to be made or an investment that should be sold." Now, while we aren't advocating one-dimensional thinking, think of this as another form of having in-depth knowledge of your business. This behavior is not far removed from that of the entrepreneur who knows all aspects of his or her business—and the competition's business—intimately.

Last but not least, says Stolper, portfolio planners need "humility because this is an error-prone business, and if they are reticent about talking about mistakes then we get disinterested." Take this one to heart. Once you lose your humility and bury your mistakes, you have become a Pollyanna.

By now you should have gotten not only some idea of the Pollyanna personality but also some clues about how to break out. Read on, because we've only scratched the surface.

Ready to pack your suitcase before continuing your journey? Be sure to take the following:

- Wake-up pills so you and your company won't be lulled back to sleep.
- Common sense so when you bring out the knife and begin cost cutting and price cutting, you apply good sense to the exercise.
- Magnifying glass, telescope, microscope, and any other optical device that will help you spot the cracks near and far that represent untapped business opportunities.

CHAPTER 3

Open Yourself to the Vision of Outsiders

"The more you know, the more you know you don't know."
—Aristotle

Breaking the Isolation Barrier

Do you still think it can't happen to you? You're wildly successful, you say. You have no shortage of good ideas. You're practically a genius. Your customers love your products, and your competition, such as it is, can't hope to keep up. Well, congratulations, you sound like a true Pollyanna.And if you think your success can't turn around and head south, then let leading portfolio manager Richard Aster feed you a dose of reality. For as this discerning investment professional knows, the cold, cruel fact is, it's hard for any company to keep up with its growth.

> You're wildly successful, you say. You have no shortage of good ideas. You're practically a genius. Your customers love your products, and your competition, such as it is, can't hope to keep up. Well, congratulations, you sound like a true Pollyanna.

"I think maybe there have been selected companies along the way that have stayed up with growth," says Aster, "but it's rare because what you find is that people feel what they need to do right now is make market share or else somebody else is going to do it, and so they're going to expand. They're going to run as fast as they can, and they're going to fill in the holes later. The truth is, companies can't grow at 30 percent or 40 percent and fill in all their bases."

Knowing this, Aster invests in growing companies, always applying his rule of thumb that "the average holding period for stock in [fast-growing] companies is around three years." The problem, he believes, is that companies do not take the extra critical step to create a strategy for growth (which we discussed in the last section of Chapter 2). "There are companies that are successful that don't make the proper strategic decisions," he says, "and this tends to really hurt them over time. They tend to defend what they're doing and, I think, this has been a major problem with successful companies."

Whether out of complacency, arrogance, or isolation, it's all too easy to lose sight of the growth path. Who would have thought in the 60s that the Baskin-Robbins ice cream franchise could be derailed by its own success? But, in fact, it became isolated from both its competition and its customers, and its efforts to regain its customer base have been a rockier road than its ice cream.

Baskin-Robbins's first error was probably its failure to respond to the changes occurring in the frozen-dessert market—both in the premium market of rich, high-butterfat ice creams introduced by Ben & Jerry's and Häagen-Dazs in the 1980s and in the healthier choice of frozen yogurt more recently. Baskin-Robbins's second mistake was to remain the kids' store, with its circus-pink interiors that did not appeal to the increasing numbers of adults eating ice cream and its many extraordinary flavor concoctions, such as bubble gum, that were not for the wider audience of customers.

It has taken 10 years, but the once-popular franchise has turned the corner on the road to recovery. Once again Baskin-Robbins is listening to customers and giving individual store managers more say in the decisions—not to mention adding a new interior design and introducing frozen yogurt and sugar-free and low-fat ice cream desserts.

Companies that expect to succeed in the 21st century need to realize that power increasingly is in the hands of the customer. Only those companies focusing on cost, convenience, customers, and communication will prevail. This wasn't always the case. There was a time after World War II and throughout the 50s when the marketplace offered fewer product choices and less competition. As a result, a company could be isolated from its customers and still grow. In fact, IBM enjoyed several decades of rapid growth in that era of limited competition. But as the marketplace began to change, it became necessary to break a company of its old habits and beliefs. In today's world, one's products are competing not only with many products made here at home but also with an increasing array of products from all over the world. This trend will only increase in the years to come.

> **Companies that expect to succeed in the 21st century need to realize that power increasingly is in the hands of the customer. Only those companies focusing on cost, convenience, customers, and communication will prevail.**

The speed of communications today ensures that your period of grace—when you can enjoy unlimited growth with limited competition—is shorter than ever. Your success and, especially, your mistakes are broadcast more quickly. The astute competitor with an ear to the ground and an eye firmly focused on you will take advantage of both your success and your mistakes.

"It's a fight to the finish," Robert Levine, the aggressive CEO of Cabletron reminds us. "It's a win-or-lose proposition. There is no in-between. That's because if you lose, your family starves." You need to know your competition and listen to your customers. But before we examine techniques for monitoring both competition and customers, let's start by understanding the source of our isolation and making ourselves more attuned to the tell-tale warning signs.

Regardless of how you feel about the politics of Robert McNamara's book on Vietnam, you should know that in it he describes a governmental decision-making policy in the 1960s every bit as isolated as that found in many companies today.* Neither President John Kennedy nor his advisers had ever visited Southeast Asia or met with more than a handful of its people. They made critical decisions completely out of context and totally removed from reality. We know firsthand the consequences of that isolation. Their decisions, made in a vacuum, affected millions of lives in this country and in Southeast Asia. When challenged either by others in Washington or by the American people, the Kennedy Administration used a tactic we've seen used in many a corporate situation: They brought in the troops and circled their wagons to defend their positions. The prevailing theory is that when people start questioning from the outside, you have to maintain the loyalty of the group and protect each other's flanks so you're not exposing the group to risk

> The prevailing theory is that when people start questioning from the outside, you have to maintain the loyalty of the group and protect each other's flanks so you're not exposing the group to risk.

The first thing entrepreneurs fighting the Pollyanna syndrome need to do is break the isolation that keeps them from focusing on competition and customers. This is never easy, because we all tend to prefer to communicate with our customers secondhand. It's easier on our egos simply to stay in the offices and boardrooms of our own little worlds. When we do talk with outsiders, typically we talk with other professionals—the retailers and distributors and salespeople—rather than subject ourselves to the direct line of fire from our customers. What does the buying public know? asks the isolated executive. The clothing manu-

---

*Robert McNamara, *In Retrospect: The Tragedy and Lessons of Vietnam.* (New York: Times Books [Random House], 1995), pp. 32–33, 321–323.

facturer gets his information from the retail store owners. The animal food supplier talks with pet store proprietors and veterinarians. And the electronics firm CEO makes decisions based on conversations with her engineers and distributors. This form of verbal isolation is deadly when coupled with the physical isolation that comes from too much time spent in our own work environments, day in and day out. We end up convinced of our own brilliance and secure in the self-deluding knowledge that we know more than our customers do. After all, we've been successful.

In an example of our own, when we wanted to help the Glen Ellen Winery, one of our clients, establish better lines of communication with its customers, we recommended the following tactic as part of an overall strategic plan: Put a direct telephone line to the winery in the wine aisle of a supermarket. This way customers could call and ask the winemakers questions. Although Glen Ellen was growing, we knew there existed among consumers a latent fear of wines. Wine can be a very confusing and intimidating product. It comes in so many varieties, colors, and flavors, with rules for drinking each with the "right" food. Wine is packaged in a bottle with a stopper that requires a special tool to open. The fact is, it's much easier just to buy a six-pack of beer.

With the direct line, customers could ask: "We're having beef stroganoff tonight. What wine should I buy?" or "Do we have to drink white wine with fish?" We discovered, however, that most shoppers were hesitant to pick up the phone. They didn't know what to say and were afraid to show their ignorance. Furthermore, the thought of anyone actually providing such a personal level of service was almost foreign. We ended up hiring a person to stand in the aisle and encourage people to use the phone.

There was equal resistance on the winery's side, which we expected. We knew most winemakers were isolated from the average customer and not attuned to the very basic problems people have buying wine. In opening up the lines of communication, we hoped to sensitize people at Glen Ellen to these issues. Yet the winemakers, too, were afraid to talk on the phone. "What do I say to them?" they asked. But eventually a few agreed to talk, and the experience was illuminating. For the first time in their careers, they heard people's questions firsthand.

We all must realize that it is very difficult to spot trouble when the market is doing well. That's why it is important to have a solid approach to overlay on the current business and strong lines of communication. But when was the last time you bought your own product in a retail store and experienced exactly what your customer experiences? If our experience with our own Holt, Hughes & Stamell clients is typical, and we suspect it is, it's probably been quite a while. We find ourselves buying our clients' products at their warehouse rather than going to a retail outlet. We all tend to limit our purchases to our own products and those of our clients. And what person in an agency hasn't received a quick glance from clients who want to assure themselves that their agency is loyally using their products. Are they wearing the client's cologne? Clothing? Sunglasses? It's not surprising, considering that purchasing a client's product is tantamount to taking an oath of loyalty. If you don't think this is accepted behavior, try to imagine IBMers buying Compaq computers. Or Coca-Cola executives drinking Pepsi. Or Kimberly-Clark employees preferring cotton handkerchiefs to Kleenex. It's unthinkable, and maybe it should be. Yet we question this practice. But more of our heresy in a moment.

Part of the solution to the problem of isolation lies in institutionalizing risk (see Chapter 4, p. 91). If you don't risk moving outside the box physically as well as mentally, you are likely to make the same mistakes successful companies have been making for years. We all know what happened when Detroit's automobile manufacturers missed their opportunity in the late 70s and throughout the 80s to give people the cars they wanted. Their success in the 50s and 60s isolated them and many of their suppliers in the rubber, plastics and steel industries from the efforts of the Germans and later the Japanese to move into the U.S. market. Detroit failed to understand why Volkswagens could ever succeed. The American carmakers didn't see how Mercedes could ever win over a loyal Cadillac customer.

But happen it has. As reported by Gabriella Stern in the August 24, 1995, edition of *The Wall Street Journal,* the once mighty Cadillac with all its arrogance and ostentation has seen its percentage of the market cut in half since the late 1970s.* Why? These once committed Pollyannas failed to talk with customers or listen carefully or believe what they heard. The Japanese, meanwhile, were doing exactly that. They asked American automobile buyers exactly what they wanted and liked in a car. And then delivered. It has taken more than 15 years, but Cadillac is finally listening. The company hopes, for example, to attract more women drivers by designing cars on a scale that fits women better and by making buttons on the instrument panel easy to operate with long fingernails. Similarly, Cadillac will offer cars in a price and style range that is attractive to first-time luxury car buyers.

It's understandable that Detroit operated under a false sense of security for several years, fueled by the fact that many Americans were slow to embrace the small car, the foreign car. But the oil embargo of 1973 soon put an end to that. Apparent economic necessity awakened people to the need for fuel-efficient cars, while Detroit slept through its wake-up call.

And Detroit is hardly alone in its vulnerability to being blinded by success. In the 1980s the Norwegian salmon industry revolutionized the availability of salmon throughout the world. In the United States, prior to the Norwegians, we enjoyed good salmon only when a friend brought back the delicacy from a trip to the Pacific Northwest. Norway created a product, created a market, and dominated the world in its production. But the Norwegians' mistake was to believe that the world wanted only Norwegian salmon. In fact, what the world actually wanted was good salmon at good prices. Consumers apparently don't care about the country of origin, as the Chileans, Canadians, and Scots have proved with their successful entry into this market.

---

*Gabriella Stern, "Car Chase," *The Wall Street Journal,* August 24, 1995, Section A, p. 1, Column 6.

Ten Ways to Know You Are Isolated

Here are 10 questions to ask yourself and others in your company. Answer honestly, because how you respond will reveal just how isolated you are from the marketplace in general and from your competition in particular:

1. In the last year, did you expose yourself to another industry or company completely outside your field?

2. Did you attend a trade show recently that had nothing to do with your product or service?

3. In the last six months, have you taken a factory tour of a company that was outside your field?

4. Did you travel outside the United States in the last year?

5. When was the last time you read a publication with a circulation of less than 30,000 that was not in your industry?

6. Have you ever purchased something from one of the home shopping networks?

7. Do you stop and talk with your company's receptionist at least once a month and ask for his or her view of the company? Or inquire as to the most commonly received calls?

8. Do you know what's going on in the local shopping mall? For example, have you noticed the increasing number of lifestyle stores?

9. Do you ever take the city bus to work?

10. In the last three years, have you deliberately bought the products of your competitors and used the product for any length of time?

If you answered *no* to at least three questions, consider yourself a budding Pollyanna; it's time to try something different. If you answered *no* to between four and six of these questions, get out of your office immediately. Seven or more *nos*? Time is running short; you probably are already beginning to be eclipsed in the marketplace. You'll have to act fast.

Need some extra credit to boost your score? List five business risks you have taken in the past year.

We must never forget that no one is immune to the isolation caused by success. Even banks, those venerable bastions of conservative thinking, were caught up in the whirlwind real-estate expansion of the 1980s. Many an otherwise cautious banker, blinded by the opportunity for profits, threw caution to the wind along with his or her money. Banks failed

Job Switch Day

Shake up the status quo. Put managers on the phones for a day. Let them talk directly with customers. Switch jobs for the day. Let employees play management. See what happens. Everyone should come away with greater insight into the problems and issues the business faces. And, who knows, you might even develop some good ideas.

to base their decisions on an understanding of the history of business and its cycles. And when the real-estate boom came crashing down, many banks and savings and loans were left reeling in the wake.

Not only is it easy for businesses to be drawn into a state of cultural isolation through past success, but they can all too easily put too much emphasis on their technology and manufacturing capability. Rather, businesses need to reach out, discuss, listen, and drive home the benefits. People aren't going to pick up on the advantages of a faster modem or a better flat-panel computer screen or bar-code scanners. It's up to companies to talk to prospective customers about benefits: the ability to get the information they want faster, the opportunity to carry a truly lightweight color notebook computer or to pass through supermarket checkout lines almost as quickly as they can push a shopping cart, or the chance to drive through tollbooths without having to stop. When people hear such specifics, they perk up. Consumers see those benefits adding to the quality of their lives.

How else do you prevent isolation after you identify it? While identifying it is certainly half the battle, now you need to open your eyes and ears and mind. You need to start institutionalizing risk. Perhaps you can introduce a risk report at your next company meeting. Challenge everyone in the company to list risks they and the company have taken. When was the last time anyone risked failure or criticism from within? What is the current status of risks taken?

Create incentives to change. Give your product away free to individuals or selected groups and ask them how much value they find in the product. Would they buy it? How much would they pay? Even something as simple as taking a video camera onto the street in front of your building and interviewing passers-by can give you a new perspective. Ask people what three things come to mind when you say your company's name. Play the video back at your next meeting. This should begin to shake up the Pollyanna in everyone.

Let us repeat: No one is immune to isolation. Remember when our own government was caught off guard in 1957 when the Russians launched Sputnik and again just four years later, in April 1961, when cosmonaut Yuri Gagarin ventured into space?

It's true that we caught up and even won the race for the moon, proving you can come back from the edge. Similarly, both Detroit (as discussed earlier in this section) and the U.S. semiconductor industry finally learned to compete against outside forces. In those last two cases, we can thank the American consumer for helping to get companies back on track. No matter how much industries have tried to get people to rally around the slogan "Buy American," people responded even more to the adage "Once burned, twice prudent."

> **As many companies have learned, playing catch-up is a serious and often expensive game. It is always harder to convert new customers and regain lost customers than to retain the ones you have.**

As many companies have learned, playing catch-up is a serious and often expensive game. It is always harder to convert new customers and regain lost customers than to retain the ones you have. Your challenge is to do everything you can to maintain your customer base, and that means listening and responding to customer needs and looking outside your company.

The Advantage of Outsiders

It's your company. You know your products, your services, and your market better than anyone else, right? Wrong. *This is precisely why you need outside help.* You probably know your own products and services too well to be objective and, at the same time, don't know your products and services in the context of the marketplace. You need the kind of help that only outsiders can bring. They can:

- Provide expertise when you need it. You can hire the best people for exactly the length of time you need them and don't have to be concerned with carrying them on your payroll. As many companies are realizing, much of the best help no longer works for corporations anyway. They have gone into business for themselves, and they are ready and willing to advise you.

The Two Sides of Outside Help

As a marketing communications company, Holt, Hughes & Stamell knows firsthand how difficult it is to venture into someone else's organization and tell management that there are some things they might want to rethink or do a little bit differently. The usual response is "You don't know our business. You haven't been involved in our industry. How would you know?"

As a manager, it's up to you to impart to your outside advisers the confidence to speak up. Don't handcuff them or make them afraid to speak up against the prevailing party line. It's the only way you will get the full worth of their talent and full value for the money you are spending.

The other side of this is for consultants to be more sensitive in their critiques. We therefore recommend that outside advisers phrase comments as questions that enable clients to see the problem themselves. The trick is to use effective communications skills to avoid issuing a direct challenge and to get the listeners to acknowledge the reality themselves. If you ask a question, the client's typical first response will be fraught with self-deception. But, in fact, most people know when they are wrong; they just need time to discover the truth. The minute they verbalize their response, they know it doesn't ring true. Giving people the room to come to the right conclusion is the cornerstone of effective outside help.

- Provide a fresh perspective because they have not bought in to your company's culture.
- Speak more honestly than most insiders because they are less likely to fear for their jobs.
- Complement your inside talent by bringing multidisciplinary backgrounds to problem solving.

As to the importance of outsiders, consider that turnaround experts virtually always come from the outside. Since you can't beat them, at least get them on your side. Our interview with Jim Shaffer, self-proclaimed newspaperman and president and CEO of Guy Gannett Communications, turned up a case in point. Shaffer understands well the role multimedia will play in the future of the publishing business. The impact is going to be something no publisher has ever faced before, because for the first time the reader will be in charge. At the time of our interview, in his effort to prepare for a time when traditional television and newspaper properties will lose ground to emerging markets and new technology, Shaffer was planning a two-day internal conference on the ethics of the new media.

"We are bringing in outside specialists from the ethics program at the Pointer Institute in St. Petersburg, Florida," he explained, "to help us with this internal dialogue. And maybe we'll add a couple of other outsiders, including an outside facilitator. Part of the object of this is to create a process for internal discussion of ethics, not because it's an isolated academic discussion but because ethics is a component of business strategy when one of the needs of the business is adaptiveness in the future . . . It all comes from seeing the long-term horizon and a need to develop a learning organization for the long term."

Whether they need an outside perspective for a day, a week, a month, or longer, smart companies are increasingly relying on outsiders to bring them the insight and expertise they lack on staff. Some have actually turned over key decisions to outsider experts. As marketing and advertising consultant Richard Roth, president of Richard Roth Associates and adviser to some of the country's marketing giants, explains, it is not unheard of today for two consultants to represent their respective client companies in some of the most critical business decisions.

> **"More and more consultants are being hired to do the thinking, and that's a function of not enough people inside the corporation, in their agencies, or anywhere with the requisite skills."**

"More and more consultants," Roth says, "are being hired to do the thinking, and that's a function of not enough people inside the corporation, in their agencies, or anywhere with the requisite skills. A lot of people have turned their back on the corporate world . . . or have been spit out by it, or both, and have become consultants. So there has been a geographical shift in brainpower . . . I believe it's better to have them outside. There is more independence of thought. And you can hire the skills you need when you need them, rather than apply a staff person simply because he or she happens to be there. You're getting the right person for the problem. Lastly, you're not supporting those people when they're not working, when there is downtime. So there are a lot of advantages to outsourcing thinking."

The most obvious advantage is that outside experts are not part of the corporate culture and are therefore less insular. Roth feels too many advertising agencies fall into the same trap as the company insiders. "I have learned that agencies tend to examine too few alternatives," he says. "They tend to reach a conclusion and then justify it. The process they pursue, or lack of process, promotes that. Theirs is not a consulting approach, usually. So, I'd say agencies tend not to deliver the optimum thinking because they haven't done it . . . And with the exception of the top people, most agency people have limited experience and limited grasp of process. For this reason, we see more shift toward consulting and outsourcing."

Roth is so convinced of the limitations in the traditional agency that he feels even such an outsider could benefit from using outsiders. He says if he were to create an agency today, he would "hire consultants as account executives. I would hire people from other disciplines as my creative people . . . In PR, for example, you probably get a lot of cross-pollination in thinking and ideas because it sort of runs across industries, and if you get people from different industries, I think you increase the knowledge bank and approach."

In fact, Roth is so certain of the need for multidisciplinary skills, he says, "I think agencies are going to become general contractors for their clients." Only in this way, he adds, will agencies begin to be paid for the value of their ideas and quality of the team they put together rather than for the amount of work they can convince a client to approve; payment will be less in markups for printing and more for the value of the ideas provided.

Smart Companies Build Smart Boards

Perhaps the most common application of the outsider is through the creation of a board of directors. Retail innovator Marshall Smith, founder of the successful Learningsmith educational retail stores and his new Cybersmith computer center in Cambridge, Massachusetts, has learned to rely on outside help. Smith's operations have become formalized enough now, he says, that "our job within the next 30 days is to try and pick seven or eight people who can do it [advise] on a more formalized basis. Outside help, that's one thing I learned from the bookstores. The bookstores I tried to do all by myself, and I can't do that. I think the major mistake that I made with the bookstores was to think that I could do it all.

I'm not a good manager. I'm a good concept man. I can motivate people. I can generate loyalty within an organization. But in terms of the day-to-day management, the organizational structure, the detail part of it, I'm not good at that."

The bookstore's going bankrupt was the painful process that brought him to his epiphany. "Financially it's a problem, but emotionally it's a disaster," he admits. He recalls a comment from a friend and professor at Harvard Business School. Smith was telling this friend about how great Videosmith, his earlier video retail venture, was going to be— this after going bankrupt on his paperback bookstores: "My friend said, 'You know, most successful entrepreneurs have gone bankrupt at least once. And when they come back and start the next venture, they're absolutely convinced that it's going to work. Then they run out of money. They can't pay the telephone bill, but they're opening two stores next month.' He described me. There I was."

> **An outside board of directors, even an informal one, is an important resource for good ideas and for a variety of expertise you may not have on staff.**

As we heard from just about everyone we talked with in preparing this book, an outside board of directors, even an informal one, is an important resource for good ideas and for a variety of expertise you may not have on staff. Hugh Farrington talks about the Hannaford board of directors: "Hannaford has a strong board today because Walter Whittier believed in that. He was the chairman of the board from the mid-1960s until the late 1970s. Walter started forming that board because he believed that the company needed to be challenged, and we needed to bring together great talent at that level of the company . . . It starts with someone with the vision to do it. I think a couple of us have been smart enough not to screw it up. He brought together top retailers, bankers, academics selected for their areas of study, such as Bill Applebaum from Harvard who was the 'guru in site location work.'"

Today the Hannaford board is composed of people with marketing and retail expertise. It is not a haven for those looking for honorary titles and some extra income. In addition to Farrington, the board includes 11 men and women who bring specific skills to the company—not merely the marquee value of a known name.

When creating your own board, you want to put together the right mix of people who can provide the range of expertise and talents you need to augment your internal decision-making process. Where do you find the right mix? Trust your instincts. Select people who can make a real contribution; people with specific skill sets. Once you start building, ask the other board members for recommendations. They will be a well-connected group of individuals who can introduce you to the right people.

> **Select people who can make a real contribution; people with specific skill sets.**

As soon as you have a board, you want to put the members to work. Trotting them out for formal events, using them to impress investors, or limiting them to the role of "yes" men and women is a terrible waste of their time and your money. If you take valuable resources and start wasting their ability, you won't be able to attract the kind of people you want in the future. Farrington explains: "We keep them [our board] involved in the front end of activities so they're not just rubber-stamping what management brings to them . . . I've found that the board is most helpful and most motivated if you bring them in at the early stages and give them a chance to help formulate direction as opposed to just bringing them in and saying 'This is what we want to do, here's the deal, say it's OK.' "

The process at Hannaford Bros. Co. is quite formalized. "We have a two-day planning session in August," says Farrington. "Those sessions are open. We will bring in strategic ideas about the company and strategic direction, but we don't bring in many conclusions. We take what we learn in August and form a three-year plan that we bring back to the board in October."

In addition, board members are expected to know firsthand what is going on, not only inside the company but in the marketplace as well, and how that relates to Hannaford's growth strategies. For example, when the company moved into New York State, the board met in Albany and drove to Kingston, where they spent part of the day in the company's new store, shopping, eating, and talking to customers. They even visited the other competitors in town. "We see that part of our responsibility as it relates to Hannaford is to make sure the board stays fresh and in touch with what we do on a regular basis," says Farrington.

Since Hannaford board members are expected to contribute, their work is evaluated almost as if they were regular employees. Members conduct a thorough self-analysis in terms of effectiveness and receive direct feedback from the board's human resources committee and governance committee.

Although the boardroom is an important source of outside vision and viewpoints, you need to guard against it turning into an extension of management. The fact is, the boardroom can be as isolated and as set in its beliefs as any faction in the company. The board also is open to the input from corporate officers. And like managers, board members are people at the top of their professions. They are just as susceptible to ego trips as anyone else. Therefore, it's an easy step from being an adviser with an outside perspective to becoming an insider who believes he or she has all the answers. It is up to you to make every effort to keep egos in check and keep board members at just enough of an arm's length that they retain their valuable perspective.

> **Although the boardroom is an important source of outside vision and viewpoints, you need to guard against turning it into an extension of management.**

The fact is, either you're an agitator for change or you're one of the group. If you were effective as an agitator, can you remain effective as one of the group? This is the ultimate challenge. Every board needs a Ross Perot, someone who asks the questions that everyone else is afraid to ask. All too often, however, the only dissension on a board takes place in committees or groups that become critical of other committees or groups—like the smoke-filled rooms of the politicos of old. In this case the candid discussions take place in the back room, seldom in the boardroom; likewise, pet issues get confronted, but many major issues are never discussed openly.

Although we have been encouraging you to shuck your Pollyanna threads, break from business as usual, and open yourself to outside influences, we have to offer one word of warning: You need to stay focused on the reasons for your change. Evaluate everything you do. Why are you making this change? Is it for the right reasons? Is it change for the sake of change, or in response to customers and competition? Even then it is sometimes difficult to direct change.

Take the case of Lands' End, the successful mail-order business in Dodgeville, Wisconsin, whose story was detailed by Gregory Patterson on the front page of the April 3, 1995, edition of *The Wall Street Journal*.* When founder and chairman Gary Comer hired an experienced mail-order executive to come in and help him establish more modern

---

*Gregory Patterson, "Bad Fit," *The Wall Street Journal,* April 3, 1995, Section A, p. 1, Column 6.

management techniques, he did so for the right reasons. Rather than fall victim to success and develop Pollyanna habits, he wanted to ensure that his company would move ahead into the new century with state-of-the-art systems and operational procedures designed to handle the needs of a growing company. According to *The Wall Street Journal,* Comer never expected the problems he or his employees would have in adapting to the new style.

Comer built Lands' End on his personal vision: "Take care of your people, take care of your customers, and the rest will take care of itself." His employees embraced this vision wholeheartedly. But their new CEO embraced a program for growth that meant doubling corporate staff, installing new computer systems, developing teams—all textbook management strategies. He built successful businesses in Japan, the United Kingdom, and Germany. He increased productivity in every department. Even in areas where employee productivity currently was satisfactory, he prescribed changes that would further increase it. What he appears to have overlooked was the existing culture; nor, it seems, could he communicate change to people comfortable in that culture.

When the CEO created a new mission statement, he emblazoned it on banners, bulletin boards, and buttons: "Turn every customer into a friend by delivering quality products, honest value, and world-class service." While the objective was not far removed from Comer's original vision, the way it was written and broadcast across the company spoke volumes to the employees. In the end, Comer had no choice but to fire his new CEO and take over full-time management again. For now, Lands' End will have to prepare for the future within the context of its culture.

Value the outsider's view. Open yourself and your company to new perspectives. But remember, too, that outsiders don't have all the answers. As a successful business, you probably have a culture and history worth preserving, at least in part. Work with your outsiders to get them to understand your heritage and the relationships with employees and customers. For in business, relationships are everything. Above all, before you bring an outsider into the fold, make sure you are committed to the prospect of change.

> **Value the outsider's view. Open yourself and your company to new perspectives. But remember, too, that outsiders don't have all the answers.**

Buy Your Competition

You have to be consumers of not only your own products and services but also those of the competition. Know what the customer (and the end user as well) experiences. How does it feel to shop in a store where your product is sold? What does the salesperson say about your product? About the competition's? How is your competition's store, service, product different from yours?

Beyond the momentary experience of going into the competition's territory, maybe you should try using the competition's products/services daily. You'll know their strengths and weaknesses. Over time, you'll find out what you love and hate about the products. You might just stumble onto some distinguishing feature that will potentially hurt your business if you don't respond. Better still, you might discover something you do better and can exploit.

As you might expect, a keen sense of the competition was virtually universal among the people we interviewed for this book. Robert Levine, the Cabletron CEO, perhaps sums it up best: "Victory. Winning. Beating the competition is a great feeling. I have enough money—I could retire today—but beating the tar out of my competition thrills me."

Perhaps this sounds a bit theatrical, but the fact is if you don't take your competitors seriously, they will beat you at your own game. Never underestimate your competitors or turn your back on them; you can be sure they have their eyes on you. And expect competition to come from anywhere and everywhere. Highly regarded marketing consultant Richard Roth defines his competition as "anybody who somebody thinks can bring them good thinking." He watches his competitors to learn who is hiring them, who thinks they are good, and who considers what to be good deliverables. "I monitor my competitors constantly," he says.

> **Never underestimate your competitors or turn your back on them; you can be sure they have their eyes on you. And expect competition to come from anywhere and everywhere.**

Similarly, sports media entrepreneur Rory Strunk identifies his competition as anyone trying to sell advertising. This broad view enables him to compete in an environment where he is not the largest player: "When advertising is bought and sold, there is a certain food chain, and we're not at the top. It's ABC, NBC, Seinfeld, and things like that at the top. But that's where we think we are trying to do something with creativity, to always be on the edge, always come up with new ideas, which moves us up a little higher on the food chain, and that's how we've been able to retain our clients year in and year out."

Although he gets most of his ideas from his own creative mind, Strunk never overlooks the competition. "I learn from my competitors," he admits. "I really use them as the learning model wherever I can apply it and look at my business and say, What is the same and what is different? Then I'll go back and I'll look at the competitors and say, What are they doing that's right and what are they doing that's wrong?"

Strunk cites lessons learned from the experiences of Christopher Whittle, president of Whittle Communications. Strunk went to many people who had invested in Whittle and asked them point-blank why they thought Whittle failed in his efforts to build a national educational cable channel. "He oversold the product to a large degree," Strunk explains, "promising things that they could not actually deliver . . . He bypassed traditional agencies and sold direct to the clients, and then when it came to review time, he was shunned by the advertising agencies to the extent that the advertising agencies felt alienated. When [the decision] finally came back to the agency, they were just waiting to can his program. It finally caught up with him." In addition, Whittle overlooked the complexities of the education arena and how to market to it in a way that both parents and teachers will accept.

It's true, as groundbreaking retailer Marshall Smith says, that it's not always easy to know what your competition is planning: "The pot is boiling, and you hope you're going to cook something that's going to work, but you don't know what's coming out of that. You don't know what the competition is going to do." For this reason, we use the term *buying your competition* in order to reinforce the active role you need to take in this process. Don't be fooled into letting your sales force be your sole source of market research. Your salespeople have an agenda of their own—an agenda created in large part by your own methods of providing them incentives. And even their best efforts to provide you with information will be anecdotal at best. Get your information firsthand. Conduct telephone surveys and, when possible, one-on-one interviews with your competition's customers.

Of course, there is an exception to every rule, and portfolio manager for the Meridian Fund Richard Aster suggests the following caveat: "I would say that I am aware of the competition. We know who they are

Assess the Competition against Yourself

You can define yourself by buying your competitors' products or marketing materials and putting them to the test. As an exercise, put your name on a competitor's products or materials and pass them out among your employees. Challenge your people to evaluate the products or marketing materials in new ways. Ask them: Are you proud to have our name on this? Would you say the same in our brochure copy? What's missing that we do better, differently? What do you see that we haven't thought to try? Why are we different? If you say, "We would never say that," why not?

A variation on this exercise is to place your marketing copy and products alongside the competition's. Again pose a series of questions to your employees: Which product best represents the product category? Whose brochure best describes the product or service? Which would you buy? Why? What is the most striking difference you notice?

Or try creating an internal focus group. Have someone describe both products without showing them to the group. Can you identify your product in such a lineup? Or have someone read both brochures out loud. Can you identify your competition in a blind test? How well have you differentiated your product from others? If you discover a lot of similarity in the answers, discuss the results.

These exercises should lead you not only to see what is special about you and your products/services but also to better understand something you may not be conveying as well as you ought. In the process, you can expect to break down some of the mental barriers and come to define your own niche more effectively.

. . . We basically know how they are doing. But I really don't let that affect the way I run the business or what I do . . . If I do a good job, the performance comes . . . I am always doing the best I can."

At the same time, he says, "We track probably 8 or 10 mutual funds that are comparable to the type of investing we do and therefore we sort of see how we do." It provides Aster with a measure to check against, not something that determines how he does business or dramatically changes the way he selects stocks. "I think we're pretty consistent and disciplined," he adds. It still comes down to sticking to what you know. You can't panic and scramble and take chances. "I think if you start watching that and let that lead the investment philosophy or style, it leads to trouble," Aster says. "It has in all the cases I've known. So I think we have a style and a philosophy that we're set in. We know it works over the long term, and I just can't worry about how other people are doing it or what they are doing."

This is true no matter what your business. Like most things, the impact the competition has on your business must be put in perspective and kept in balance. You need to develop a good plan. You need a lot of historical data from which to develop your ideas and strategies. Then you must follow your decisions. "For successful investing you have to have a solid strategy," Aster says, "and you have to have the judgment and the ability to execute the strategy. You can examine yourself, but it comes back to the basics."

Earlier we said that we question the conventional wisdom of loyalty. Using, buying, or even making the effort to understand the competition's products is often seen as the ultimate act of corporate disloyalty. In 1963, David Ogilvy wrote, in *Confessions of an Advertising Man,* that he always used his clients' products. He drove a Rolls-Royce and bought his clothes at Sears (and, we might add, still made the Best Dressed list). This was his way of proving his loyalty. Twenty years later, he reinforced this point in his *Ogilvy on Advertising:* "It is bad manners to use products which compete with your clients' products."*

While there is some merit to Ogilvy's position, we suggest an important codicil: The ultimate loyalty might just be to use the competition's products and report on that experience to your client. Loyalty is not making your client feel good; it's giving your client honest information and new perspectives.

Company loyalty is based on telling the truth, not on telling what the boss or the client wants to hear. It requires being honest even when it hurts. It's up to management to minimize the risks. Loyalty on management's part may be to listen and not respond, just think over what was heard. There'll be plenty of time for talk later.

We're not saying the "company way" is completely wrong, and it's definitely understandable. Nor do we expect it to change unless word and example come down from top management. But neither you nor your employees nor your suppliers are learning anything new by avoiding the competition. It's up to you to create a safe environment that encourages people to try different things.

---

*David Ogilvy, *Confessions of an Advertising Man* (New York: Atheneum, 1963), p. 56; and *Ogilvy on Advertising* (New York: Vintage Books, 1983), p. 61.

Perhaps McCann Erickson, the agency with the Coca-Cola account, should serve Pepsi or RC Cola to all visitors in its offices, then ask them how they liked it. How does it compare with Coke? What's their experience? Then the agency could pass this information on to the client. It sounds impossible, doesn't it? Alas, probably 99 percent of companies play it safe and stick to their clients' products.

One word of advice, however: If you decide to defy the corporate culture of a client and wear or use something other than the client's brand, do so blatantly. Say, "I bought this XYZ brand computer, and let me tell you why. Let me fill you in on my experience after having used it for two months." Loyalty, in our opinion, is doing everything in our power to serve the client, including providing competitive reporting. We believe you should develop a partnership with your client based on honesty.

On the flip side, as a client, you need to realize you can't control every product in a consultant's office or home, so at least get some value out of that person's experience. Similarly, instead of telling employees they must shop in the company store, encourage them to collect outside experiences. Being loyal only to your products is ultimately being disloyal to your company, because by being loyal in this fashion to your company, you may end up going under.

Talk to Your Customers

We hinted earlier (p. 72) that there is a difference between a customer and an end user. An end user drives the sale and has impact all the way up the line. A customer is someone who buys a product or service from you that may be repackaged into a consumer product or service. While you must consider your immediate customer, you must also understand the end user, the final customer. A shoe manufacturer, a wine producer or distributor, or a candy manufacturer—each sells to a retailer. The retailer is the manufacturer's customer but not the ultimate user. If you're the manufacturer, you can't listen to the retailer alone. Find out, too, what the end user wants and thinks. Think of ways to ensure that the final customer is happy with your product or service beyond what the retailer does; you can, for example, put out special information, educate the consumer, offer guarantees. Glen Ellen did this when it agreed to test a direct supermarket "hot line" to the winery in California (see again p. 59).

You can learn from your customers, even if you learn only what they don't know or understand about your product. You'll create a bond with the ultimate customer. You'll also create a bond with the retailer (your other customer) who likes the fact you make his or her sale easier.

Sports media entrepreneur Rory Strunk doesn't have an outside board as yet. He plans to move in that direction during the next couple of years. In the meantime, he relies on what he calls his informal kitchen cabinet: his customers. "I talk to my clients," he says. "I talk to them about successes. I talk to them about failures. I use my clients as a real good backboard. That's probably why we have clients for such a long time—because there's a real sense of partnership there."

> **You can learn from your customers, even if you learn only what they don't know or understand about your product.**

The customer is always right. When was the last time you saw that on a sign hanging above the cash register at the checkout counter? In theory, every person in business knows the importance of the customer. In practice, well, that's another matter. The prevalence of poor customer relations is precisely why we've all learned to put up with bad service. And it's not all the bad attitude and poor manners of the kid behind the counter. Business owners, in their isolation, can be just as negligent toward their customers. The results are some business decisions by even smart companies that leave you scratching your head.

How else can we explain Time Warner's decision to introduce fiber-optic cable in Maine by announcing to people that there would be a $3 charge added to their cable bill? The switch to fiber optics would benefit people, but the people didn't know that because Time Warner failed to generate a need. The company failed to create demand and build excitement for the benefits of fiber optics prior to installation. Rather than getting customers to practically drool, the company ended up with a revolt on its hands and had to rescind the automatic monthly charge. In the end, Time Warner heard the customer loud and clear and gave them a choice.

In their eagerness to create the first low-smoke, low-tar "healthy" cigarette, executives at RJR Nabisco went ahead with plans and never bothered to inform the board of directors formally. The directors, when they did learn of the secret project, were furious. But soon they had a lot more to worry about, namely, who would control the company. Cigarette research proceeded, with two camps of executives and directors polarized over the decision to introduce the new cigarette that, as many said at the time, was known to "taste like s——!" No one was thinking about the customers. The customers, however, had the last word: They refused to buy.

Portfolio manager Richard Aster has made a study of his clients—both those he keeps and those he loses. The results enable him to understand more about customer habits and his business in general. "You're going to lose clients consistently for a lot of reasons," he explains. "Sometimes you do very well for a client, you make them a lot of money, they decide to take the money and do something else with it. Sometimes there's mergers, there's acquisitions, sometimes you may have a bad spot in performance that they're not willing to tolerate. The year 1987 was a bad period when we had the crash. A lot of people felt the easy decision then was not to be in small stocks. It was safe to go back to the Big Board or to whatever and say, 'Well we're safe, we're in big companies'. . .

"We have had people from the very beginning, and I would say these are people by and large who aren't financially oriented on the market every day . . . They've seen us through the good and bad times and they have confidence that it's going to work out over a period of years. I find if you can get through a few years with clients and do a good job for them generally, you keep them a long time."

Investment manager Michael Stolper has made his own analysis of customers and has come to some surprising conclusions about service as a niche. From his own study, Stolper has a better idea which clients he should accept and which he should avoid: "We went back and did studies of attrition, and I could not find a pattern where there were high levels of ritual contact with the clients . . . There was no difference in attrition between those that I have frequent contact with and those that I have virtually no contact with. I thought that was important . . . It was my conclusion that while a lot of client service has to do with the notion that people want to see you and that they somehow want to integrate you into their lives, the fact is most don't. Certainly we have high levels of discussion when things aren't going right, but otherwise they sort of forget about us. They know we're out there. They know we're responsive, but they're not interested in seeing us at frequent intervals . . . I think a lot of service marketing or client service has to do with assuaging the insecurities of the vendor rather than really being a requirement of the consumer. It's absolutely at odds with what everybody will tell you about a service business . . .

"What the attrition study demonstrated was that something like 80 percent of attrition occurred in the first 18 months of the client relationship, and the conclusion I reached was essentially that you get certain people who come in and 'top-tick' cycles. In other words, you tend to get an avalanche of new business coincident with inflection points in the market. Even though you tell people, at least we do, that they are probably not going to make money for a while and very likely they will lose some money before they make any, they don't want to know. So they hire an investment manager, and the market rolls over a year later and they are down 12 percent and decide that equities are not for them, or we're incompetent or whatever. They process it different ways, but essentially they conclude that it was a mistake and go away."

While this information hasn't changed Stolper's investment philosophy or process, he admits: "We have, however, become better about declining new business. We probably decline half the people we talk with just because we think their expectations can't be gratified over time . . . It is, in fact, a nonlinear business, and they want to believe that it's linear. So we feel the best decisions we make about new business are the ones that we decline."

By studying your market and your business and customers in a microcosm, you may not find yourself changing any aspect of your business, but at least you will be equipped with the understanding of why it works. Whether you conduct telephone interviews, focus groups, customer forums, or surveys, you have to know the customer's mind. "Find out the interests of the customer," says Cabletron's Robert Levine. "Discover their hot buttons and focus on them. Have conversations with other people in the organization you are trying to target and ask them what are the hot buttons. Ask the person you are selling. Find out as much as you can and use it to your advantage."

> By studying your market and your business and customers in a microcosm, you may not find yourself changing any aspect of your business, but at least you will be equipped with the understanding of why it works.

You can put the Internet to work in your efforts to communicate with your customers. An ever-increasing number of on-line forums, private chat rooms, and on-line auditoriums make it more practical and cost-effective to reach large numbers of current customers and prospective customers. And testing ideas on-line can give you a quick cross section of market reactions. You can conduct an on-line survey for a fraction of the cost of a telephone or mail campaign.

The information you collect can help to keep you from becoming isolated from the marketplace. And as you explain your ideas to people, you will have an opportunity to see firsthand what benefits captivated your audience. Armed with this knowledge, you can better fine-tune your product ideas for market. You'll also know which concepts and benefits to promote in your advertising and public relations campaigns.

Levine believes in building a relationship with his customers: "Ethics with customers are very important. You have to build up trust with customers if you are going to prosper." One way to keep your business focused on this relationship is to include the customer in your mission statement. We know that sounds obvious, but it's more rare than you might think. Businesses typically put their emphasis on their products, service, technology, and manufacturing ability. The customer, in practice, ends up last.

Try constructing a mission statement from the perspective of your relationship with the customer rather than from the perspective of manufacturing and technological capability. If your goal is to "promote technology and increase revenues," you're going to have a harder time than if you recognize that your goal (without ignoring the bottom line) is to "create a business-customer relationship." Our previous example involving Time Warner and fiber optics is a case in point. The cable company appears to have focused on the technology and lost sight of the customer benefits.

By now you should be practically embracing your customer. This is about the time we like to introduce some contrary advice, and here it is: Customer opinions need to be balanced with your own vision and knowledge. Customers, albeit critical, are just one piece of the puzzle. You need to consider your competition, technological potential, global market, and especially your own creativity.

Besides, people don't always do what they claim, so you need to keep customer comments in perspective. They tend to give the answers they think you want to hear or to say what they think they should do. The fact is, New Coke tested well, but it has never been the national success story the company expected.

Sometimes, too, as we've mentioned before, customers can see only as far as the world they know. They will not typically be your source for revolutionary ideas. The truly innovative breakthroughs typically come from visionaries such as yourself. Customers could not have told Motorola the value of a beeper, or told Compaq to create PC networks, or recognized the value of the fax machine. You have to find a balance between what customers want and what your vision tells you is right. This doesn't mean you shouldn't test new ideas on customers. By all means allow them to offer you their perspective as you refine your products, but keep in mind the need to balance their vision with your own.

As you can see, there is much to be learned outside your office walls and away from industry biases. Gathering this information is only the first step. You need to sort it, study it, and apply it to your business. And in the last analysis, you need to combine it with the best ideas within your business.

Ready to continue on your journey? First, pack your bags with a few more critical concepts:

- Value the outside perspective to get a fresh view of your business.
- Avoid isolation at all costs.
- One way or another, you'll hear from your customers. It's better to ask for and listen to their responses than hear the sound of receding footsteps as they walk away from your products and services.

CHAPTER 4

Defy the Corporate Culture

"I have not failed. I have merely found 10,000 ways that won't work."
—Thomas Edison

It's OK to Fail

You can defy your corporate culture; it's not really as radical as it sounds. It's not like we're asking you to defy authority—the mantra of the Woodstock Generation. This is not a rebellion of defiance but rather a revolution of the mind, a revolution designed to change the thinking of everyone in your company, from the CEO to that summer intern you hired six weeks ago. It's a revolution intended to develop employees who think like owners. Just as the best renters are those who act like property owners, the best employees are those who treat their job and their company with the same care and attention as the business owners. By defying your corporate culture, quite simply, you will come to create a new environment in which everyone in the company has the confidence and security to speak up and share thoughts and ideas.

If loyalty, as we defined it in Chapter 3, is about honesty, then defying the corporate culture is the process that *enables* loyalty to exist. Although it's a simple concept in theory, it's going to require considerable effort from management and employees alike. Management must take the first step in creating an environment in which all employees feel comfortable in speaking up and know that they won't lose their jobs just because they told the boss something he or she didn't want to hear.

> **Management must take the first step in creating an environment in which all employees feel comfortable in speaking up and know that they won't lose their jobs just because they told the boss something he or she didn't want to hear.**

The challenge is to make every employee a stakeholder by creating an environment for doing business in which the opportunity to discuss is open to everyone. In addition to feeling safe, employees must believe their thoughts and ideas will be taken seriously. The new corporate culture requires that everyone learn to listen, discuss, then act—in that order.

The first step toward defying the old order is to understand failure by realizing it's not exactly what we were taught in school. Just as success can engender failure, failure can lead to success, provided you have the right attitude. "Success is 99 percent failure," said Japanese manufacturer Soichiro Honda. Failure is less a stigma or symbol of defeat than a part of a process. This is why we advocate the celebration of mistakes.

Our fear of failure is natural, coming out of the years of emotional and psychological baggage we all carry. Everyone pays lip service to learning from their mistakes, but how many of us practice the concept faithfully? Schools set us up from the beginning to loathe failure. Success in the form of good grades was our ticket to graduation and a good college. Mom and Dad certainly never praised our flops. And probably every boss we've ever had lacked the understanding and vision to see the progress in failure.

"To be successful," Cabletron's Robert Levine—who readily admits he plays to win—told us, "you need to look at failure as a motivator. You can't win every deal. Take what you learn and move on. If you have allowed failure to become defeat, then you won't succeed. Motivation, not defeat, is the key to using failure to your sales advantage . . . You have to get back on your feet again. Ask yourself, 'Why didn't I win this one?' Figure it out and move on. When I miss a sale, I can't wait to get on to the next one so I can win it. It's like golf: Do you want to end your day on a good shot or a bad shot?"

Sports may actually provide a perfect analogy to help put failure in its proper new perspective. Baseball players calculate their batting averages in terms of the number of "at bats" they have. They know they're not going to hit a home run every time or even drive in a run. But the more trips they make to the plate, the more opportunities they have for a hit. And when they foul out or strike out, they've at least had the chance to learn something more about the pitcher. With that knowledge, their chances of getting a hit the next time are improved.

In business we often take the opposite approach. Paralyzed by fear of failure, we sit on the sidelines second-guessing our products and strategies. As a result, we often miss opportunities in the marketplace and the chance to learn more about consumer buying habits and market potential. Rather, we should take calculated chances and strive for as many "at bats" as possible. When we don't hit the grand slam, we can't just retrench. We must rethink our strategy and next time at bat apply what we've learned as we swing for the stands, and maybe we'll connect and knock the ball right out of the park. Remember, we've got to *play* the game to win. The real trick is to make errors faster than the competition so we have more information and more opportunities to win. This is the key to turning failure into success.

Convert Failure into a Game

Use the same approach as athletes. There is always another race, another game, another time at bat. Make it the same in your business. Learn from your mistakes, then go back out and try to hit the line drive or throw the touchdown pass. Change the lineup. Bring in a new pitcher. Try a different play or redesign your product. Build up your muscle where it will do the most good. Become stronger and more agile. Put more depth on your team. It's OK to fail so long as you learn and move forward with the knowledge.

Some of the greatest failures and fiascoes have led to success and good fortune. For example, the failure of a certain glue to stick permanently, as its inventor had hoped, led to the creation of 3M's Post-it notepads, perhaps the most widely acclaimed intrapreneurial corporate effort in history.

Let's look at a couple other examples in more detail: The Macintosh computer didn't become a success overnight. After Steve Jobs and Steve Wozniak achieved initial success with the Apple II series of computers, they introduced two comparative failures back-to-back. The first was the Apple III, which was a beefier version of the Apple II. It was larger and more cumbersome than its predecessor and never as popular, but it enabled the company to make its first inroad into the business market. The Lisa was a complete departure from the past and the true precursor to the Macintosh. It was larger than the Mac and very slow, but it introduced the graphical user interface that was to revolutionize the industry. Together, the Apple III and the Lisa legitimized Apple as a computer company.

Jobs and Wozniak did one other thing that distinguished them from the crowd. They planned for the company's future by making their own product obsolete. The Apple II series was still selling well when the Mac first appeared. Over the next few years, as the Macintosh began to find its way into homes, offices, and particularly design studios, the Apple II became the educational tool of choice. And because schools were so wedded to the Apple platform, many chose the Mac when it was time to upgrade their computing power. In fact, it has taken years for IBM to capture a significant piece of the secondary school market.

Similarly, at first look, Federal Express's short-lived entry into the fax market in 1983 with Zap Mail—one of the first commercial fax services—appears to be a failure because the company pulled the service less than a year after its introduction. Zap Mail succeeded, however, in helping position the company as a truly global player in the priority delivery business. With Zap Mail, companies could transmit documents to FedEx offices around the world within minutes. This, coupled with FedEx's acquisition of Flying Tiger, which already provided international delivery, helped give the company the international image it has today.

Zap Mail failed largely because Federal Express was unable to launch its own satellite, which the company believed would make the fax network cost-effective. Of course, with hindsight we know that even had the company received approval for a satellite, the explosion in the personal and office fax market eventually would have limited the long-term success of FedEx's fax service. But out of this apparent failure has grown a priority overnight delivery company that others emulate. Today, private air courier services control more than 90 percent of the market. According to *Traffic World*'s figures of March 1994, FedEx has 34.5 percent of the market, followed by UPS with 21.6 percent. The next closest competitor, Airborne, has less than 10 percent. The U.S. Post Office's Express Mail service has just 4 percent of the market.

Now that we've seen how failure can lead to success, let's look at examples of how fear of failure can lead, ironically, to failure itself. Ask yourself why a U.S. company didn't introduce the compact disc player. If you say it was because we didn't invent it here, you're wrong. U.S. companies were paralyzed into inaction by twin fears: On the one hand, they feared the product would flop because consumers were not ready to give up tapes and records. On the other hand, what if it succeeded? Companies were afraid to supplant their existing technology with something that might kill the market for tape players and turntables, older technology that was still selling. Alas, it's thinking like this that has enabled Japanese consumer electronics companies to beat us with our own technology.

And consider the irony of IBM. For all its market troubles during the past decade and its reputation for not being a market leader, IBM today probably holds more patents on technology than any other single U.S. company. Whether because the company is paralyzed by fear of failure or unable to see the commercial application of its inventions, IBM

Beginning of the Ad Campaign:

"And I think, gentlemen, you'll agree that we've simply but eloquently captured the essence of the proud, noble heritage of whatever the hell it is you people do up here."

is seldom the first to market. There are signs that IBM is changing; but to make the transition to leading-edge innovator, the company may need to institutionalize risk as corporate policy.

Consider the difference between the typical private investor's approach to the market—which is to avoid loss at all cost—and that of the professional portfolio manager or Wall Street trader. At Salomon Brothers, for example, it was always William Salomon's philosophy that the best way to learn what was going on in the market was to jump in and do some buying and selling. Maybe the investors wouldn't make money the first time. Maybe they'd even get burned. But they would know more the next time. They'd know who was buying and selling. They'd have a better idea of what the market would bear. Conversely, when the market goes down

End of the Ad Campaign:

*"On the other hand, gentlemen, when you turn the chart
this way, it reveals an entirely different picture."*

or a stock or bond doesn't pan out, private individuals tend to focus on the loss and often retrench by getting out of the market or investing more conservatively. The professional typically takes the new knowledge and applies it to his or her next trade or investment.

The next time you are in the middle of a great failure, stop and think of all the ways it could have been even worse. A trade-show manager told us about a show he ran for the Latin American fishing industry that was a failure on paper because it lost $40,000. Yet the organizations involved in the trade show had projected losses as great as $100,000. When the show lost less than half that projection, coupled with what the participants gained in market knowledge and exposure, the show's promoters pronounced the event a success.

Move beyond Failure

If something fails, our first thought often is to get rid of it, wash our hands as quickly as possible. Rather than abandon a failure immediately, you should move beyond it only after you spend time looking at it from all angles. Try to gain an alternative perspective by opening your problem to new audiences. Talk with outsiders. Discuss your idea at a cocktail party. Make your failure a case study for a marketing class at a local college or university.

To ensure that your employees are involved in the process, collect advice from people at all levels. Perhaps circulate a survey across the company: What could we have done to prevent failure? Is there still a market we are overlooking? Let them answer anonymously. Get feedback from the people closest to the problem; encourage their honesty in a safe environment. Ask them, "Where can we go from here, knowing what we know now?" Ask everyone to make a list of problems or obstacles and compare them with missed opportunities and with what the competition is doing. You may discover new possibilities.

Look at your failure and ask, "What about this effort makes me proud?" You may find many successes in what first appears to be a failure: The product is superior. We didn't lose as much as others did. We gained a toehold in a new market sector. We have begun the process of developing a new niche. We are now associated with being a player in a new niche or industry. These are all worthwhile outcomes, and as long as the failure leads to ultimate success, you can celebrate your mistakes.

Related to the fear of product failure is the employee's worst nightmare—the fear of being fired. A senior manager we know wishes to dispel that fear permanently: "Being fired was the best thing that could have happened to me," he explained. "It allowed me to make the move I had wanted into my own business. We think playing it safe is going to make us more secure; but the fact is, that kind of behavior adds up to poor performance. After I was fired, I asked the president, 'How are you going to manage the department while you look for my replacement?' No one had a plan, so I came back to him on Monday with a proposal—printed on letterhead I created on my computer—to help the company throughout the transition. The point is, I put my firing in the past, drew up a list of

Bury the Past, but Don't Forget It

If a product is a complete disaster, sometimes you need a technique for shaking off the failure and getting it totally out of your system. You can get yourself and your employees over the hurdle by holding a mock funeral. Have an open-casket party and bury the product. Start with a large box (your make-believe casket) and invite everyone to put in products, reports, documents, research—whatever they associate with the failure. Then cremate the remains and put the ashes on the shelf as a pyric victory, and a reminder. The emotional issues have been laid to rest, but the ashes will sit in your office serving as a visual reminder that you don't want to make the same mistake again.

things they needed to do short term, and ended up working for my former employer part-time during the next couple of years, making several times my original salary. The company went through four division managers before they found my permanent replacement, and I worked for them off and on throughout this period."

If you want to be really proactive, create a contingency plan for yourself. Determine what you would do in the event you are fired. Our own experience with employees is that a firing, no matter how painful, seldom comes as a complete surprise to the individual. Often it can be a relief to an employee in over his or her head but afraid to let go. We've actually had employees thank us for helping them make a decision they couldn't face. You'll be in an even better position to carry on if you have considered the possibility and created a plan for yourself.

Once everyone in your organization understands the real role of failure, the company can move toward the next, and most critical, step: institutionalizing risk.

Institutionalize Risk

What we are about to suggest will mean potentially opening a Pandora's box in your workplace. Once you have given people the opportunity to speak up and have said, "We admire you for being in our face," you have to be prepared for what follows. We feel what follows is worth the conflict and discussions you will be unleashing. And as you read this section, remember that employees will always complain, if not to your face then behind your back. It's better to get issues (and ideas) out in the open than to have people wasting time grousing and saying things that bring down everyone's morale. If criticism and complaints and ideas go unheard, that's potentially money lost that could have been applied to a new opportunity. In the end, your business is about making money. Institutionalizing risk is not some touchy-feely exercise; it makes good business sense.

> **Institutionalizing risk is not some touchy-feely exercise; it makes good business sense.**

Just as your outside consultants and agencies should be encouraged to bring their experiences to the table, so should your employees. Making risk safe is the oxymoron we use to describe freeing employees from an environment of fear and control. You need to encourage groups to speak up, and you especially need to encourage younger or newer employees— those least comfortable with speaking up—to share their ideas.

If you recognize the value of having a diversity of ideas and cultures on staff, and are hiring people from different fields and backgrounds, then the time to start tapping into their thoughts is sooner rather than later. Get to them while they are new, because what they have to say during their first couple of months, before they become insiders, will be most enlightening. You should consult new employees regularly and submit them to an extensive posthire audit within six weeks of their joining the company. Get their thoughts before they become immune to the uniqueness of your business. You will never have a better chance to see your company through fresh eyes. At the same time, you are creating a precedent by encouraging them to speak out early.

So how do you begin to create mechanisms whereby people are rewarded for speaking out and taking risk? How do you show them it's safe?

Change has to start at the top. Management has to be willing to have employees in its face saying how they feel about issues. Guy Gannett Communications CEO Jim Shaffer says he relishes working with a diverse group of people who speak out. He told us that, while it is easier to be an autocrat, strength lies in diversity of experience and ideas: "If I work with people who are all of one mind, we end up as a group with a strategically dysfunctional process of groupthink . . . I've been trying

Pick Your Best Resource

Here's a little test: You are seeking advice about merchandising your product line. Which employee from the list below do you feel will give you the most valuable advice? (Circle one.)

1. Someone who has a thorough understanding of all aspects of your business and respects its position in the industry.
2. Someone who has a thorough understanding of your industry, but only your industry.
3. Someone who knows very little about your industry but has a wide range of marketing and sales experience related to new-product launches and product repositioning.
4. Someone who will be able to tell you exactly what you want to hear.
5. Someone who has worked for your biggest competitor.

Number 1 sounds like a Pollyanna to us, and Number 4 is the proverbial yes-man, whom you don't want. The other three all have roles to play, but if we could select only one, we would pick Number 3. Why? There is little question that employees are more valuable when they know the competitor's business, but because everyone in your company should already be making efforts in this direction, Number 5 would not necessarily add anything new. We also assume you already know a lot about your industry, so Number 2 may be redundant. Therefore, your best bet is to hire someone who knows products and merchandising and can bring a fresh perspective to you and your business. This is the true value of diversity.

You don't want to try to apply the cookie cutter to your people. Different personalities, different talents make a company strong—even in top management. The CEO who is a visionary, for example, will most likely be the antithesis of your chief of operations. As Hannaford Bros.' business-savvy CEO Hugh Farrington explains, "If you have sheer value as the base, which is integrity and honesty, then you can allow for all these differences above the line . . . Get the baseline, then get the right characteristics for the job above that line."

very hard to create an environment where divergent thinking is tolerated, even if I staunchly disagree with it. If the views are strongly felt by talented people, I damn well better listen."

Management's task must be to spread the gospel to all employees by practicing what it preaches. If you are going to institutionalize risk, you have to stand by that position and not humiliate, punish, or fire employees who stand up to you and present ideas and actions you may not always agree with—particularly if their ideas or actions lead to some failure along the way. Include your human resources people in the first wave of change. They need to understand what you're planning so they can support the effort throughout the company.

There are seven steps you need to follow to institute change and begin to institutionalize risk. The following paragraphs describe these steps in detail.

Step 1: Management must accept that there is such a thing as good conflict. However, to make this a positive exercise, employees need to understand that while it is important to fight for what they believe, they can't become so emotionally involved that they take the fight personally. Business battles are not meant to be taken out of the conference room. Good conflict occurs at very honest moments, when people are brave enough to express differing opinions. This type of positive conflict leads conversations to a more evolved state and builds stronger relationships between coworkers.

Step 2: You need to develop a dialogue throughout the company to show employees that risk is safe (the oxymoron we introduced earlier in this section). Of course, you need to develop a happy medium between unstructured nurturing and getting the business to run smoothly and profitably.

Hannaford's Hugh Farrington has instituted what he calls experimental research and development to facilitate employee risk taking. "We have a food court in our Kingston, New York, store," he explains, "the only food court that we have in the company. It's not working. But we made a decision to go ahead because we needed to understand firsthand whether we should or should not be in that business. Intellectually we felt we shouldn't be in the business, because we're not Burger King and we're not McDonald's . . . But a lot of people in the retail food business are doing this, so we needed to experiment.

"It's costing us money, and that's what should happen. There is probably less entrepreneurial experimentation but more corporate experimentation going on today . . . So we are still experimenting. We still feel the need to push forward, but I would say it is more institutional than entrepreneurial."

Step 3: The definition of loyalty extended to outsiders must also apply to your employees. True loyalty is knowing something the boss doesn't know and having the courage and conviction to share that information. Pepsi television ads to the contrary, Coca-Cola employees are not secret converts to their competitor's soft drink. But they probably should be drinking it regularly. In most companies, this is still viewed as heresy. If you work in a supermarket, that's where you shop. But consider the value of encouraging employees to shop the competition and learn how other stores operate. Imagine the advantage of having employees come in and say, "I went to Acme Market over the weekend and their shelves were poorly stocked, I stood in line for 15 minutes because only two checkout counters were open, and I had to bag all my own groceries." Or the contrary: "I've never seen so much choice on the shelves as when I went to Acme. And their state-of-the-art bar-code scanner at the checkout counter had me out of the store in seven minutes. Not only that, someone actually carried my bags to the car!" In either case, both you and your employees will have a better idea of how your company compares, and you can all start to do something about it: promoting what you do better, fixing areas where you don't measure up.

Step 4: Develop a team mentality. There is no limit to what you can accomplish as a team to improve your ability to compete.

There is no limit to what you can accomplish as a team to improve your ability to compete.

To build a team mentality, invest the time and money in a "Team Day," moderated by a professional, to explore intracompany relationships. Devote a staff meeting to a discussion of the vital importance of each person's contributions. Once a month, put work aside to allow for a few hours of fun and relaxation together. These small gestures pay off in priceless teamwork and a smoothly functioning company.

Step 5: As you begin to create a new, more open and responsive corporate culture, make certain that each employee's goals and the review process you use match what you are saying you expect. If the means by which you measure an employee fail to match the message you are sending out, your bid to change will fall on deaf ears. No one will

A Simple Way to Encourage Risk Taking

Telling people to take risks is never enough. You must show them and show them often—in large ways and small. For example, ask employees to list three mistakes they made this week or month. Then ask them to describe the lessons they learned. This is a simple reminder that mistakes will be tolerated as long as lessons are learned.

risk a poor review just because you have asked employees to speak out freely and take more risks. If you're going to institutionalize risk, you have to commend employees and promote them according to their ability to take calculated risks, to be honest, and to give and accept constructive criticism. By matching your rewards to your message, you'll be dangling the one carrot that will cause employees to change their beliefs.

Step 6: You can help foster diversity within your company by looking for opportunities to rotate people among different jobs. Job rotation reduces insulation and encourages a more open perspective. Of course, not everyone is equipped to do every job. But if you look, you'll find good matches. People not only will have a better grasp of other jobs but will also see things they can do in their own job to make another job easier and improve the business overall. For example, have an order-entry person swap jobs with the order filler and send the order filler to the loading dock. Together, the three of them might surprise you with a way for cutting two days out of the order-fulfillment process. Or they might discover that orders headed for the retail store are packaged and repackaged several times before they leave the warehouse. They might then figure out how to save time and packing material, which cuts waste and helps your bottom line.

Step 7: You may have personally bought in to the philosophy of risk, but your employees may still hold the perception that the company doesn't want them to take risks. This often explains why self-directed teams break down and turn into work groups led by one person, a supervisor, who tells everyone else what to do. People feel uncomfortable grabbing responsibility. If this is the case, you have only completed half your job. You may believe in risk and want people to speak up, but you haven't made it clear to your employees. You haven't institutionalized it yet.

Focus on the Journey, Not Just the Destination

The journey is as important as the process, as the executive director of the Maine Audubon Society, Thomas Urquhart, learned. In the Spring 1995 issue of *Habitat,* he wrote about his experiences traveling by rickety bus (called *bache*) in West Africa to visit his daughter in Mali. The 100-mile-plus trip from Mopti to Djenne took 20 hours. In the course of the trip and all that transpired, Urquhart awakened his senses to all facets of his adventure. "In committing myself to the unpredictability of transportation in Mali," he wrote, "I had made a conscious decision to shake off the habit of considering only points A and B and never the time and space and experiences possible in traveling between them. Djenne might be my destination, but getting there by bache would be no less interesting." He concluded by saying, "It is hardly surprising that something so different should shake one up so profoundly."*

While you don't need to go to West Africa to rattle your mental cage a bit, you need to look at all your business experiences with fresh ideas. You need to find the value in the experiences along the way to your destination. As you move toward your objective (to change the corporate culture), keep your eyes open to the little changes and experiences along the way. You'll appreciate your progress more, and you might just uncover some stumbling blocks and barriers that will make getting to point B easier in the future.

---

*Thomas Urquhart, "The Road to Djenne," *Habitat*, Spring 1995, pp. 3–4.

If you can institute risk, you will see a difference in your company tantamount to the difference between painting by the numbers and letting go on a blank canvas to create something truly great.

Of Missions and Visions

In your quest to change employees into "owners," you can raise buy-in by inviting them to participate in high-level planning. Many people question the long-term value of business plans and mission statements (more on that later), but there is no doubt that developing these documents is a valuable exercise that goes a long way toward giving employees a vested interest in the company's success. We suggest taking the

Challenge Business as Usual

Make everyone responsible for a question that challenges the way you do business. These are not to be personal swipes at management but legitimate questioning of the big picture. Until people feel comfortable speaking up about big issues, you probably will want to make this an anonymous exercise. The responses are turned in, then posted on the wall for the week prior to your next staff meeting. At that time, each question will be answered and the answers dissected. Who knows, the next big idea may come out of a simple question. And you have certainly made strides toward fostering a community in which people can come forward with new ideas and question old ways freely.

formalized, traditional process, usually reserved for top management, and making it participative and fluid. Make your plans and statements living documents that bind your employees together.

In terms of helping you plan exactly where the business is going or where it will be in six months or two years or five, a business plan is not very accurate or helpful. Meridian Fund portfolio manager Richard Aster puts very little stock in business plans. As he told us: "No, I don't have any specific business plan, and it's hard to make one in our business . . . because it depends a lot on market cycles, which I can't predict. We find that, for example, if we have good performance for a year or so, we'll get a lot of assets in. If we have bad performance for a year or so, we may lose assets. So in terms of a business plan and adding people and adding products and so forth, I don't have any real long-range plan. My basic plan is really to do a good job investing."

For much the same reason, premier investment manager Michael Stolper doesn't talk in terms of business plans but rather contingency plans. "When you've been around a long time," he says, "there are certain things that you know. You know that the economy grows about 3 percent a year; and if you're growing a business at 20 percent a year and you have high margins, then it's only a matter of time, in a competitive world where the barriers to entry are relatively modest, before you're going to attract very stiff competition. The net result of this is your growth rate will diminish and your margin will get pinched.

"Now let me get this straight. You have <u>no</u> 5-year plan?"

"That you know. What you don't know is how long a roll you'll get . . . Since day one, we've had contingency plans to determine, as business turns, how to start taking costs out of the system with the least amount of damage to the long-term health and culture of the enterprise. Our compensation schemes are reflective of that. We emphasize relatively modest current compensation with huge bonuses that relate to both individual and collective success of the enterprise. I have a depression mentality, and anytime somebody asks me a question, part of my response is going to be to say, 'This is great, but what happens when markets break?' No, I think contingency planning is essential."

Likewise, the problem with so many mission statements is that they are written to be as broad as possible, ostensibly to allow for every conceivable opportunity. In the process, they often become verbiage that means as little to people inside the company as to people outside. At the same time, as Stolper says, vision statements are "a useful ritual to encourage focus." If the process is handled correctly, employees at all levels are able to focus on the big picture.

Whatever your approach to business planning, you can create a big-picture exercise that involves employees. For our purposes, therefore, the issue in this chapter is not "Do you or don't you have a plan?" but rather "How do you use the planning process to keep the company moving forward and your people completely in sync with your objectives?"

Jim Shaffer, CEO and president of Guy Gannett Communications, developed a strategic plan in 1993. He shared it with employees in the summer of 1994. "There's no rocket science anywhere," he admits. "The trick is to stay with the strategy." And that requires employee buy-in: "It will take time, and obviously our employees have to participate in it, and they'll have to help us develop these strategies. It starts with us explaining the strategy and then asking for their input and setting up a common scoreboard from which everybody can watch the score. The structure of our strategic planning will be to develop a shared consensus on priorities and criteria for success. Anything that comes from the minds of six-figure executives, by and large, is going to be sterile until people at all levels, particularly people who interact with the customer, start to believe. And it's going to take years to sell that process, and the vision may change. If the process works properly, the visions probably will change. It won't just be Moses coming down from the mountain with the stone tablets. Moses comes down with a draft and says, 'This is what I'm thinking right now; let's start talking about it.'"

Whether you're developing a business plan, a mission statement, or vision statement, there may be many specific ways to get to the goal, and all of them may be worthy of pursuit. For this reason, we suggest you let the public relations people develop their plan; manufacturing its plan; production, accounting, sales, and creative people their plans; and so on. We borrowed this concept from the supercomputer, which supports massive parallel processing. As with the supercomputer, all these processes working alongside each other can do more and do it more quickly than one large linear system can.

Your business plan needs to be fluid enough to allow for new ideas you might not have considered—especially when it comes to technology—at the time the plan was created. As Rory Strunk, creator of the innovative Resorts Sports Network, explains: "It's funny—our decision to go onto the Internet did not come from a business plan right off the bat. It came from a sense that there's an opportunity here that could be a great planning opportunity for an all-sports network. Let's do some R&D in Texas, we said. Once we get some feedback, then let's do a business plan . . . Sometimes business plans are very consuming. Sometimes it can take a lot to get input. Sometimes the marketplace is moving so fast you've got to at least react in some form or fashion and then get enough evidence to do a business plan. Anybody doing a business plan on the Internet, I guarantee you, is being outdated almost on a daily basis. Business plans do give you a road map, but they are not the guiding plan you need."

The process can be serendipitous for a while. But eventually, as Strunk says, you need some sort of a road map. "We have a master plan, and that's where we developed the concept of 'extending the value chain,' " Strunk adds. "So we have a vision. We say, 'OK, here's our product. We're in the content business. Content is "being" in this media world. So how many ways can we distribute our content?' That definitely has a vision to it. And the vision changes as the market changes. OK, that's our vision, to extend our programming. What distribution avenues do we have? Who are the partners? How do we go about it? We change almost daily because of huge upheavals in the media world—with cable companies and telephone companies and the utility movement . . . It seems every day we have a new way of accomplishing our goal. So those aren't written in stone, but we have a vision for where we want to go."

Company leaders need to have vision, but they also need to institutionalize their vision so employees can develop the procedures and operations that really are manifestations of the leader's vision. We asked Strunk to describe how he extends his personal vision to employees as a whole. His reply: "You convey the perseverance to your employees by outlining a very clear vision to people and saying, 'OK, this is what we want to go after.' Having them be a part of that vision and having them

> "Business plans do give you a road map, but they are not the guiding plan you need."

Commitment versus Compliance with the Corporate Vision

In 1994 at Holt, Hughes & Stamell, our management met first to discuss and develop a collective statement of our corporate vision. But we knew the six-month process was only half complete. We needed the input of everyone in the company in order to ensure that employees were committing themselves, not merely complying with some vision handed down from above. We had, after all, attracted a set of employees who had agreed to join our firm based in large part on what they saw and what we said to "sell" them on our business. Their perception of that vision was essential.

Our methodology was interactive: We began by writing everyone's vision on the marker board. Next we sought commonalities. Gradually we pieced together a vision statement that satisfied both management and staff and, we felt, quite accurately captured the essence of the firm.

Because we developed the vision statement with the help of the whole agency, most employees are committed and share a sense of ownership in our statement. Of course, as we continue to grow, we'll have to revisit our vision many times in order to retain employee commitment and buy-in.

have input in that vision will give them perseverance. Because they feel like they're investing in something, they're putting something on the line . . . A technique I support is real openness—having an open-door policy to new ideas. Everybody is treated as equal in the company. There really isn't much hierarchy. Equity too; if these big projects or big visions come to fruition, employees will have a vested interest when they bear fruit."

To keep on track, you will want to revisit your mission and vision regularly, particularly during the fast-growth years, and especially while you are adding new employees. Not only do you need to ensure that the mission matches the realities of the marketplace, but you also want to continue to keep employees in the loop. And a plan or a mission or a vision written prior to their being hired will not have the same importance for them as it has for older employees.

Finally, just as with your attempts to institutionalize risk, you need to tie employee goals and performance measurements to the plan. You must judge people based on their ability to live up to the vision. If you fail to make employees' goals reflect the mission and vision, you'll create chaos and confusion. You can't have one mission and vision but another measurement structure. It's like saying your company's goal is to deliver the best possible customer service or to create products friendly to the environment, then telling your sales force to focus on moving product or your field reps to double the number of clients they service each week. If you change your measurement structure to be in line with your goals, then people will serve the mission. Don't expect them to take something that's written on a piece of paper and act on it if they are still being judged and measured according to older standards. Then after you match vision and measurements, visit the branch offices to see if the message there matches your corporate mission/vision as well.

Defy the corporate culture and you will be on your way to creating a powerful working environment. You've made the first step toward changing attitudes and creating a new context in which Pollyannas will have difficulty surviving for long. Your business will be a force to be reckoned with in the industry.

Not once in this chapter, until now, have we used the word empowerment. That's not because we don't recognize the role empowerment has in defying the corporate culture. In its purest form, empowerment is probably a lot of what we are talking about. However, in the past few years many companies have talked about empowerment but failed to create the corporate model to back it up. The revolution we're advocating is not to be confused with the program-of-the-month mentality employees have come to equate with more talk than action. To allow employees truly to defy the corporate culture, you first need to change the way you do business internally, thereby enabling employees to contribute the best of their talents.

Open up your flight bag and add this next set of rules:

- Don't be afraid to talk about and learn from your mistakes.
- Get serious about taking risks. Encourage everyone to speak up and participate in the give-and-take of discussion. If you are the boss, now is the time to become comfortable with this critical process.
- Get everyone to commit to, not just comply with, a vision.

CHAPTER 5

Here Today, But Are You Gone Tomorrow?

"If it ain't broke, we've still got a chance to fix it."
—Mike Hammer

If It Ain't Broke, Break It

If you want to really cut to the heart of any lingering Pollyanna attitudes and static thinking, start by assuming that everything about your business in the past has failed. Of course, this requires the ingenuity and willingness to look deep at the current state of your business—internally and externally, including any threats to your product lines from either competition or other outside forces. It takes honesty and a complete lack of arrogance to admit your most successful product or even your business itself might not survive. It's a process of reinvention that begins with contingency planning that not only will position your company for continued growth but might also save it from extinction.

How do you reinvent your business? As we said above, begin by assuming everything you've done has failed. People intuitively analyze failure, not success. If you make the supposition that everything you've done has failed, then you'll be applying the same type of analytical thinking and analysis to everything you do—success and failure alike. In short, you'll be celebrating your successes as if they were mistakes. As a result, you will be less likely to subscribe to business as usual or to make unsubstantiated assumptions that just keep you going along the same path. Rather, you will come to learn from your successes the way you should already be learning from your failures.

Always remember, the Pollyanna syndrome exists in a world where everything appears to be going along nicely, even though there may be undercurrents or outside influences that could bring you down. By celebrating your successes as failures, you will be forced to take the status quo apart and maintain an edge. Today you stand at the crossroads. Either you can subscribe to the Pollyanna mentality that change is something that happens to you, or you can make change happen proactively. If you are going to make change happen, you need to institutionalize some type of thinking that will enable you to stay ahead of the curve. Otherwise you have to wait for some outside force to make an impact on your business, and that could be devastating.

But change requires a reason, a rationale. It's not something you do simply because it's about time to try something new or just for the hell of it. Planned change is a process built on a continuum. It shouldn't be radical, unless you've been wallowing in Pollyanna complacency for years. But be prepared for a few aching muscles because, like any exercise, it's tough when you first begin. Each week, each month you stick with your program, it becomes easier, until it's part of your routine.

You won't actually reinvent your company or products on a daily basis. But by remaining open to the process, you will be mentally alert and able to accommodate the demands created by new markets, new technology, and new customer requirements.

Why is this important? Because the impetus for change has never been more urgent. Not so long ago—sometime in the late 70s or early 80s—the world experienced a second Big Bang. It wasn't physical, like the creation of the universe, but its impact has been every bit as critical. We're talking about the Technological Big Bang, which is transforming our world at an astonishing pace. The impact of this high-tech explosion on change has been more than an incremental acceleration. It has caused discordant, discontinuous, virtually random change. It's also hard to manage because we never know when change is coming or from where.

> You won't actually reinvent your company or products on a daily basis. But by remaining open to the process, you will be mentally alert and able to accommodate the demands created by new markets, new technology, and new customer requirements.

Not only is change now seemingly unpredictable, it's difficult to keep pace with its increasing rate. With the dawn of the industrial revolution, only about 200 years ago, the economy began to shift from agriculture to mass production—a transition that lasted more than 50 years. Two entire generations had time to adjust their attitudes and develop a new way of living and working. Today we are bombarded by technological change at a pace where six months equals a technological generation. We have only months to adapt or be left behind. This is what your company and its products are up against. You have smaller windows of opportunity in which to make your initial move into a market, and you will have to reposition your business more often.

Meridian Fund's portfolio manager, Richard Aster, speaking from his perspective of watching companies for potential investments, marvels at today's growth cycles: "In the old days, if somebody had a new product, a new idea, a new concept, he may go on a year, two years without competition. Today, with venture capital money, if anything looks promising, there's going to be five start-ups within six months. So the life cycles, the product cycles are very short; the competition is intense."

To compete requires us not only to observe change but also to have the knowledge necessary to implement change. One distressing fact is that, according to the National Science Foundation, in 1992 the United States spent less on nondefense research and development (1.9 percent of the gross domestic product), than either Japan (3 percent) or Germany (2.7 percent).*

As Aster acknowledged, while the rate of change is rapid, the best investment strategies are still those that rely on picking "good companies." This is what you want to aim for: to be a company that doesn't give in to Pollyannaism, is always adaptive, and is not afraid to reinvent itself as necessary—a company that balances competition and customers with a vision for the future. Keep your eyes and ears tuned to the world around you, establish flexibility in your planning, and remain open to new possibilities.

Dinosaurs Don't Have Vision

Ask yourself some questions: What would have happened if IBM hadn't existed? What if Henry Ford had never been born? Would we be living without computers? Or cars? Of course not. Not only did IBM *not* invent the computer or Ford the car, but other companies would have filled the gap and brought those or similar products to market. At the same time, these companies were led by men of vision. Thomas Watson, Jr., saw the opportunity to revolutionize the office machine market by reinventing his father's business. Henry Ford envisioned making automobiles affordable and used the assembly line to mass-produce his vision.

While entrepreneurs have vision for creation, they also need a vision for sustaining their companies. They must see beyond their initial success. This second vision comes, in part, from watching the competition and listening to customers. It also comes from keeping your vision tuned to solutions, not products. Consider the fate of carbon paper and the companies that made it. If those companies listened to customers, as many no doubt did, their focus was on making a cleaner product (such as chemically treated paper) or one that simplified the process of fixing mistakes on copies. It's hard to imagine a single secretary or office man-

---

*Statistical Abstracts of the United States, compiled from the National Science Foundation, "National Patterns of R&D Resources," annual; and Organization for Economic Cooperation and Development.

ager attending a focus group and saying, "Forget carbon paper and fix your sights on photocopiers." As we said at the end of Chapter 3, customers rarely have the broad vision needed to change an industry. At the same time, they have the ultimate power to drive change once new technology or products are offered. By adopting the new products offered by competitors hungry for your share of the market, customers can effectively leave you behind. Your task, therefore, is to apply your vision and knowledge in order to remain a leader, not a follower.

> **Customers rarely have the broad vision needed to change an industry. At the same time, they have the ultimate power to drive change once new technology or products are offered.**

So what do you do? You learn from the past, you look to the future, and you try to apply change to your business, wherever you see the need. In short, you prepare for the inevitable. It would have been hard for us to imagine just five or six years ago that personal computers would become so pervasive as to become commodity items. Yet today we willingly buy computers from new, no-name companies that beat the name brands in price and performance. Similarly, could you have predicted that accounting, a venerable profession, would become a commodity service? Or that professional accountants, caught in a highly competitive race, would be trying to figure out how to market their services and add new capabilities, in short, to reinvent themselves? And most recently, the rise in HMOs and other efforts to keep medical costs affordable is beginning to turn doctors into interchangeable technicians.

It's only been since the 1960s that photocopiers fairly effectively killed the carbon paper business. Yet today, just 30 years later, the photocopier faces a similar fate. Don't believe us? Well, the technology exists today, and it will happen. We actually are closer to the paperless society than you probably think, which is particularly hard to imagine since copiers and computer printers have increased paper usage during the last decade or so.

But with a computer, software, adequate disk storage, and an optical scanner you can kiss the photocopier good-bye. At the same time, you also gain greater flexibility. With this desktop system, you can scan documents and make copies through a laser printer. You also get the power to store the documents in the computer and view them on the screen. There

Play the Dinosaur Game

To begin preparing yourself to look at the world and your products a little differently, select three popular products or services and create possible extinction scenarios for each. Once you start seeing the world around you this way, you can more easily focus on the future of your own products and services. Then it's only a small step to creating a contingency plan for your own survival.

goes the future market for file cabinets! With optical character recognition software you can even convert scanned documents into text files. And while you're at it, get rid of that stand-alone fax machine because you can scan and transmit documents through your computer and modem to any fax machine or other computer with a modem. This is precisely why you see companies like Xerox and Wang Laboratories beginning to describe themselves as document companies rather than copier or computer companies.

Now let's take the post office, a real dinosaur in the making. Since the mid-1980s, this butt of our jokes and source of so much frustration has been discussed as a potential candidate for privatization. Had this action been taken then or earlier, the post office might be different today. But as we know, the U.S. Postal Service has lost much of its parcel business to UPS and other carriers and most of its overnight service to Federal Express and UPS, who together deliver about half the overnight mail. Compare that figure with the one we cited earlier for the post office's Express Mail—only 4 percent. At the same time, much of the business correspondence has moved to fax. Many companies still back up their faxes with hard copy delivered by mail or Federal Express, but increasingly we are accepting fax machines as the primary means to deliver letters and documents. This leaves the post office mostly with bills, junk mail, magazines, and greeting cards. But even this fact is changing.

Electronic banking gradually is reducing the number of bills you pay through the mail. How many of us currently make mortgage payments through a direct withdrawal plan? How many of us receive the option of direct deposit for paychecks? Automated teller machines are an important step toward electronic banking, helping us become confident that our money is relatively safe. Some banks already are offering banking by phone, and with the advent of smart cards, credit cards will become reusable debit cards. As we pay more and more bills electronically, there goes another primary source of revenue for the post office.

The Internet and other on-line services not only make E-mail a viable alternative to the post office but also have the potential for providing cost-effective direct mail. Of course, for E-mail to supplant mail, everyone will have to be connected. Some estimates have 1 billion people connected on-line by the year 2000. That's one-eighth of the world's population, and even if these numbers are overly ambitious, it is coming, and quickly.

Mainstream and alternative magazines, newsletters, and newspapers are already experimenting with on-line delivery. The industry has even coined a new term, E-zine, for these on-line publications. Not only are printing and postage costs eliminated, but these publications can offer subscribers opportunities to customize the product. Once on-line, users can select from a menu to request only the information they want. Entry costs are so low that, for all intents and purposes, anyone can create an E-zine.

Even the greeting-card business is changing. You may already have become comfortable with the computer-generated Christmas letters you write and receive. Why not send them via E-mail too? You probably will, soon enough. Today, you can send a Hallmark card via America Online. True, once you create your personalized card on-line, Hallmark still sends the card through the mail. But as the universe of connected homes and offices grows, this too will change. Soon enough, you will create a personalized card on-line and send it via E-mail. The "zap" approach will win out in the end. In the meantime, card companies are trying to keep the conventional card business healthy by offering high-tech cards featuring sound chips that play Happy Birthday and recordable voice chips for delivering a personal message. But as the Hallmark experiment on America Online proves, greeting-card companies are looking ahead to the next generation.

So how is the post office preparing for what appears to be the inevitable? There is talk about more computers to monitor and speed delivery. The post office may even be looking at E-mail and other on-line technologies, but with the government pulling its financial support for the Internet and thus, leaving it open for commercial vendors to vie for control, we have to wonder if the post office isn't a prime candidate for extinction. In the meantime, in an effort to increase revenue, the post office has been promoting stamp collecting. With the introduction of television advertising for new issues and even a catalog—which brought in more than $1 million in sales in the first six months—stamp collecting has become a multibillion-dollar business for the post office. For now anyway.

It may be hard to imagine, but local libraries and bookstores may disappear. With truly portable wireless computers, we may download our books from publishers and libraries, paying a fee for the content. The handwriting appears to be on the wall. Already local libraries are making their card catalogs available on-line to schools and homes. And the Library of Congress has a site on the Internet. You can buy CD-ROMs containing collections of classic literature, which have the added benefit of being easy to search. Even the complete *Encyclopaedia Britannica* (all 32 volumes) is available on Britannica CD. And in an era of shrinking municipal budgets, how can libraries continue to afford new books and the extra space to shelve them? But to become a viable alternative to books, the pocketbook computer must become durable and extremely lightweight, with long battery life and screen technology that is as easy on the eyes as the printed page.

Now let's take our line of thinking to the extreme. As we begin to eliminate paper, so goes the highlighter business. Are companies like Swan Stabilo seeing the potential for their business dry up someday? What are their choices? Can they focus their core business on the task of highlighting and create computer highlighters, similar to the way some companies have gone into the computer equivalent of Post-it Notes? Or do they focus on manufacturing plastic tubes? Could they become syringe manufacturers? Or straw manufacturers? Or do they find an entirely new application for markers? The choice will be theirs.

Finding new applications is a challenge that requires a focus on solutions. Several years ago, Arm & Hammer, for example, faced with the reality that fewer people were baking from scratch, gave new value to baking soda. It's long been known that baking soda kills odors, so the company built a campaign that recommended people put a box in the refrigerator and another in the freezer to absorb odors. Then, the ads said, when the box has been in the fridge a few months and you are ready to replace it with a fresh one, dump the old box down the drain to make that smell fresh too. Not satisfied it had saturated its market niche, this clever company went even farther. It created a series of personal hygiene products with baking soda—toothpaste, mouthwash, and

The Curse of Capital Investments

In the 1800s, the United States adopted steam technology and heavy machinery at a rate that far surpassed that of England and most of Europe. Why? We had far less capital tied up in aging machinery and labor. Our machines were mostly wooden and our need to compensate for a smaller labor force enabled the United States to justify the cost of new equipment and new processes. Today we see this same type of phenomenon occurring in Pacific Rim and many third-world countries. Even with vision, this is a difficult challenge for companies to overcome. It will take all our commitment and creativity to invest in the future at a rate that will enable us to keep pace.

deodorant. By redefining uses for its original product, Arm & Hammer has produced a whole new line of consumer goods.

By focusing on solutions, companies can even move through periods of transition unscathed. Take fiber-optic cable. We all agree that fiber optics are better than copper wire for sending voice, data, and video transmission. But the technology is probably not the future long-term. Satellite technology is more economical, except for one thing: The United States has a tremendous investment in its cable infrastructure, probably making it more cost-effective for U.S. companies to go the fiber-optic route first. The best companies, those focused on solutions rather than products, no doubt see satellite transmission in the not-so-distant future but will start with fiber optics and will profit. In the meantime, as less-developed countries that lack our established infrastructure move forward, the same companies will go there with satellite technology. Already there are places in the world where cellular phones are more prevalent than in the U.S.

As you prepare your company for the future, your vision is essential because sometimes life will throw you a curveball that brings with it change from unforeseen forces. For example, Ocean Spray has effectively used the media to create a year-round, worldwide market for cranberry products. But the U.S. cranberry growers have been hampered in their efforts to keep up with growing demands from consumers for cranberry juice, and for the last few years fresh cranberries for the holidays have been difficult to get in some areas. For one thing, U.S. environmentalists have stepped up the protection of wetlands, which includes the bogs where cranberries are grown. But as we've said before, look for opportunity in the cracks. Today, Chile is beginning to supply much of the demand for cranberries in Japan and Europe.

Future Watch

While you don't have to be a futurist on the scale of Alvin Toffler to forecast the future of your products, you do have to be open to the possibilities around you. Above all, as we emphasize throughout this book, you can't be blinded by your past success. You have to expand your view of the world for your product and keep your vision sharply focused on the forces that prevail. We've talked before about the need to watch your competition. But how broadly do you define your competition? If you are in the airline business, for example, is it the other airlines? Is it the Concorde? Perhaps charter flights? Or economy flights? Virgin Air? Yes, but not exclusively. As Southwest Airlines CEO Herb Kelleher knows, it's Greyhound. It's charter bus companies. It's automobiles and high-speed train lines. It's cruise ships. We might add that it's even teleconferencing, which allows you to do business without leaving the office. Kelleher positions and prices his airline services with all these alternatives in mind.

> **"If you have defined a niche for your business, you must take care not to limit your view of the competition only to other companies in your niche."**

If you have defined a niche for your business, you must take care not to limit your view of the competition only to other companies in your niche. When watching the future, you need to get out of the box that is your niche. For example, you probably go to trade shows to market your products and services and to get a look at the competition. We asked you earlier if you ever attend trade shows outside your industry. If you don't, you are missing an important opportunity to see all your competition. Fish Expo, for example, is ranked among the top 100 trade shows in the world and targets the global fishing industry. You can see the whole industry displayed vertically and horizontally under one roof.

As long as you limit your horizon to your immediate industry, what you don't see are the barriers you have created for yourself: You are part

Key Word Search

If you are looking for fresh ideas and new contexts for your products and services, try a key word search on the Internet. You may be surprised at the topics that come up. You may see connections between your products and services you never considered before. Or try setting up an on-line forum to discuss your industry. With so many people on the Internet from different backgrounds and different countries, you may get an interesting conversation going that will give you new perspectives or trigger your thinking in new ways. This is one more way to help get Pollyanna out of the groupthink mode.

of the groupthink. If you are a seafood distributor, you can't limit your competition to other seafood companies. Your biggest competition may be coming from a worldwide trend away from fish—maybe toward poultry or beef or vegetarianism. If you rely on your industry trade show alone, you will have a myopic view of your field of competitors.

As a top executive with more than 25 years of experience in newspaper management, Jim Shaffer has become attuned to change. He described the changes facing media, particularly the shift from distribution to content, as follows: "Right now, we have reporters who gather the news. They feed it into computers. The computers set type, the type goes onto pages, they get printed . . . [In the years to come] we're going to separate the information gathering from the distribution, so the media company of the future is going to have maybe three tiers. It's going to have information gathering, a multimedia information database, and a marketing group. The latter will take data from a common source and market it in different ways. Some of the marketing groups will be conventional newspapers. I would be very surprised if there aren't people who still want news presented the way it's being presented now. Maybe this part of the organization is always going to be seen as, for example, the *Portland Press Herald*. But the information that goes into the *Portland Press Herald* is going to come out in other forms as well. This is being done now.

"The *Casco Bay Weekly,* one of our competitors, went on the Internet. No big deal; there are 75 dailies on-line now. But when we started studying what the *Casco Bay Weekly* was doing, we discovered they had in one classified category 75 seasonal rental ads on the Internet and only 7 or so in print. So they've done two things. They've gone from a weekly to a daily and gone from regional to worldwide. So now if somebody in London wants seasonal rentals on the coast of Maine, they can get it from our competitors better than they can get it from us. That's like ringing a wake-up bell.

"So information gathering will be reportorial, and what we now call classified ads and other forms of ads will go into a database, and we'd better start feeding it out. I hope the *Portland Press Herald* continues to evolve as a newspaper, but more importantly I hope the resources that we're using to generate information can be used for other purposes . . .

"How do we compete with the 20 million [information resources] that are going to be out there? We're going to try to create a brand identity for our program and content family so that it's like Sears was in the 50s . . . [with] a certain guarantee of quality, like the Good Housekeeping Seal of Approval. I think in a world of media anarchy, we can add value with a brand identity for program packaging, which the individual operator is going to have a very hard time doing. We have to set a gold standard for credibility . . . But notice what's happening here. Power is shifting. It used to be if you had . . . distribution—electronic or physical distribution—you had power. Now the power is shifting toward content."

> **Power is shifting. It used to be if you had . . . distribution—electronic or physical distribution—you had power. Now the power is shifting toward content.**

Having the vision is only half the equation. It's not enough for Shaffer to see the change, or to even realign his business objectives. In preparing for change, he has to take steps to prepare employees. Changes in areas this deeply rooted are likely to create problems inside an organization. Shaffer explains the challenge he faces at Guy Gannett Communications: "The ethics of television and the ethics of newspapers are not the same. The news people are now feeding a multimedia database that is going to go off in different directions . . . Skilled people, valuable people are saying basically, 'Hell no, we won't go.' That's a sign that we need to talk . . . They understand this is going to change the company, and some of them don't want it to change. It's my job to keep the company changing with the world. It's also my job to keep their energy in mind and flowing in a positive direction because

The Progress Curve

How quickly do people pick up on new ideas? Jim Shaffer says to imagine a bell curve as your rule of thumb: Whenever you present a new idea, expect something like 6 percent of your listeners to come to the conclusion before you—the true visionaries. Another roughly 8 percent are fast to grasp the point and become advocates. About 36 percent soon jump on the bandwagon, while another 36 percent drag their feet but grudgingly agree to go along. Acceptance then drops off at the same rate, with about 8 percent never accepting the idea and 6 percent that try to sabotage it.

they have the strength." Shaffer's plan for a two-day internal conference (mentioned before on p. 65) for all employees is part of an effort to help everyone through these issues and to enable them to move into the future.

Most owners of fast-growing companies reach a time when they face the Y in the road, when they have important choices to make and questions to ask: Should I go for broke and try to build my company into a global competitor? Do I have the stamina and deep pockets for the fight? Can I compete against the big boys? Should I find a venture capitalist willing to stake me in exchange for a piece of the business? Or should I look for a Fortune 500 company with the resources to take my company to the next level? Have I accomplished all I can? Should I sell out and move on?

To answer, entrepreneurs must conduct an honest assessment of where their companies are going and how they will get there. This includes auditing their resources, their ambition, and their personal capacity to meet the challenge of growth. The story often goes like this: An entrepreneur has a great idea, which serves as the content for creating a new business. In its first years, the company grows quickly. But sooner or later it faces a challenge from other, often larger, competitors—with deeper pockets, national advertising, and more clout on the supermarket shelf. While content is king, until the Internet and other on-line services become more widely distributed, conventional advertising can make or break a product.

More than one company has seen the handwriting on the wall and sold out to a larger business—taken the money and run, so to speak. Three entrepreneurs with new ideas for a line of soft drinks formed Snapple Beverage Corporation in 1972. In late 1994, they sold Snapple to the Quaker Oats Company for $1.7 billion. The verdict is still out on whether this will be a great deal for Quaker Oats and whether Snapple can compete effectively against Coke and Pepsi. Quaker Oats at least appears committed to the challenge—as demonstrated by its launch of a highly visible national advertising campaign. At the same time, Coca-Cola Nestlé Refreshments has an aggressive advertising campaign for its Nestea brand targeted directly at Snapple iced teas. It's doubtful that the Snapple founders, with $700 million in annual revenues at their peak, could have competed in this arena.

The Benziger family of Glen Ellen (Sonoma County), California, created a popular line of fruity, varietal wines under the Glen Ellen label. They did this with virtually no vineyards of their own—only 60 acres set aside for their superpremium Benziger label. Rather, they bought grapes from others and became masters of marketing and distribution. At their peak, the Benzigers sold only about 3.5 million cases a year. Realizing they had gone as far as they could, in 1993 the family sold out to the British distributor Heublein, retaining only their Benziger premium label.

In making your decision to sell or not to sell, you have to consider the trade-offs. Ben & Jerry's ice cream, for example, has not sold out to a larger player. It has also stalled with sales of around $150 million, in part because the founders were slow to adopt the low-fat trend. The decision to bring in an outside president suggests they want to try. But in Ben & Jerry's case, their social and environmental agenda may be as important to the corporate vision as the ice cream itself. Our idea is merely supposition, for only Ben and Jerry know their heartfelt vision. They may very well be content to have their company remain a smaller player with an aggressive social plan.

Eddie Bauer, on the other hand, chose growth and a global marketplace over the cracker barrel. While mail-order giant Spiegel has been able to provide the venue, and while the company's sales passed the $1 billion mark in 1993, this expansion came with a price tag. Eddie Bauer, once the L. L. Bean of the Northwest, has traded in its original image as a specialty outdoor outfitter to become a casual clothing retailer.

On the other hand, L. L. Bean has been very careful to protect its image and equity. It has remained true to its original vision for more than

Operation Future Watch

When trying to introduce new ideas, our tendency is to study, report, polish, and generally overengineer the process. To stimulate an open attitude toward change in your company you may want to try the following: Assign a committee or even one person to watch and report on future trends. This does not preclude others from bringing their ideas and insights to the group, but it does give you at least a constant flow of information.

To stimulate discussion, your future-watch committee should present observations at staff meetings. After a new concept is posed, invite your staff to break into groups and spend 15 or 20 minutes discussing and brainstorming. Then they should come back together and share ideas for another 10 or 15 minutes. These short spates of brainstorming will keep everyone in the process and add life to your staff meetings. The process also encourages people to think on their feet and not get bogged down in committees.

80 years and turned down many offers to expand. The company has, of course, rebuilt and greatly expanded its store in Freeport, Maine, and has even opened stores in Japan. But it has been very cautious and conservative in its expansion plans. It has clung to its image and its reputation for quality, value, and customer service. Today there is almost a mythology about L. L. Bean's customer service and the policy to take back anything.

Then there's the hamburger chain White Castle, which has not grown as quickly as it might have and rarely updates or adds to the menu. In pure dollars and cents, however, White Castle is successful. The company is growing at a rate of about 10 new restaurants a year and has yet to saturate the market. In a sense, White Castle has remained true to its vision too—hamburgers for a largely working-class audience. It has new markets yet to enter and has not rushed blindly forward in an effort to mimic McDonald's or Burger King.

There is no right or wrong answer when it comes to addressing change, only a need to stay alert. But be prepared, because it will take all your efforts to understand the main forces at play: your customers, your competition (all your competition), technology, legislation, socioeconomic change, and your potential for growth. Then take your observations and information and test them against your vision. If you can do all this, you're fighting the Pollyanna that dwells within. And you will be as prepared as possible to adapt.

Rules for Reinventing Yourself

Typically businesses and people don't focus on reinventing themselves until they hit trouble. It is easier to do this when you have bottomed out because you have nothing to lose. Richard Nixon reinvented himself twice. After he lost the presidency and the California governorship, he went back and repositioned himself. Then after Watergate, he came back as an elder statesman. But we really should learn to reinvent ourselves and our businesses while we are still successful rather than waiting until we are in trouble.

> **We really should learn to reinvent ourselves and our businesses while we are still successful rather than waiting until we are in trouble.**

Just as unforeseen change can kill a company or its products, seeing what's coming not only can help you survive but also can provide you with a plan. The following are seven rules we created to give you the power to build a contingency plan.

Rule 1: Practice Revolution, Not Evolution

When you spot a trend or get a new competitor in your sights, you can't prepare your company for the challenge by using scissors and glue. Try, and you'll end up patching together a Frankenstein monster. Rather, be decisive. Cut your ties with the past. Even if you have been a success since the day you started, you want to remain open to transformation. Changing a company is not like getting a haircut and telling the barber to just take a little off the top. You have to be prepared to change your style altogether. If you have a crew cut and the market dictates it should be a Mohawk, don't think you're going to keep up with the fashion by just cutting a little more off the top. If you want to have impact, reinvent.

This is precisely what Jack Welch has done at General Electric. His rule is to be number one or number two in every field, or get out of that business. As a result, he didn't try to salvage poor-performing segments of the market; he sold them.

We can find a parallel in the current debate over term limits. In an effort to prevent politicians from becoming too entrenched, many people now believe the solution lies in limiting the number of years a person can serve in office. But this precludes a good politician from continuing to serve the people. It also ignores that we already have the power to vote someone out of office. What Congress needs is a good dose of transformational thinking—perhaps in the form of an amendment to the Constitution that raises the minimum age for entering office. Minimum ages set in 1792 were created when people lived, on average, only into their 50s. It wasn't unreasonable to allow a 25-year-old to enter the House of Representatives or a 30-year-old to run for Senate. In 1792, most 30-year-olds or even 25-year-olds were established business and professional men. They were not professional politicians. To ensure that most future politicians, good or bad, have careers before going into government, perhaps we need to change the rules and force them to do something prior to running for office.

As you plan for your business transformation, however, don't expect to change overnight. The radical behavior is in the decision making, not in the implementation. Create a plan for gradual change rather than plunging into perpetual chaos. Phase-in change much the way Jim Shaffer is preparing for the future of Guy Gannett Communications—by understanding the implications, starting to redefine the organization, and educating staff for the transformation.

Rule 2: Focus on Solutions, Not Products

Because you don't ever want to become so wedded to products or services that you don't know when it's time to kill them, your best bet is to focus on the solutions your company provides—some might call this *core competency.* For example, Canon makes laser engines for printers and photocopiers. Motorola, among other things, provides communications solutions. In fact, while both companies market their own brands of photocopiers and cellular phones, respectively, they also are multinational providers of these solutions to other companies. They have effectively divorced themselves from the end products to focus on broader solutions.

Time Warner sells cable services. It also sells satellite dishes. At the other end of the spectrum, the company owns and distributes content

Lights, Cameras, New Action

Consider the early days of the movie industry. Today we think in terms of special effects, lighting, angles, and camera movement. But when the industry first began, movies were plays captured on celluloid film. The actors came from the stage. It took more than a decade for film people to begin experimenting with close-ups, lighting, fade-outs, and multiple camera angles.

The movie industry might have moved forward even more quickly had its executives assumed that everything about the theater had failed and broken with conventional thinking. The trouble with theater, they should have said, is that everyone has to sit, which provides only one perspective on the performance. People can't get up, walk up on the stage, and look the actor in the eyes. Is the murderer in this story telling the truth or not? Let me look him in the eyes.

Today's media include the on-line networks and interactive, multimedia computer programs. Their development, ultimately, will gain little from past assumptions about television or even early computer programs. Hyperlinks, for example, allow content developers to abandon the constraints of linear thinking. Rather than developing Internet information to duplicate a corporate brochure on-line, we can provide information in selectable chunks that more closely resemble the way people think and process information. Users can just read an overview or can get more information when they want it. Interactive television may be moving in much the same direction, giving users control over camera angles and which sports plays they want to see in slow motion, instant replay. It is the viewer's choice.

So when you look at the potential for a new technology or a new medium, assume the old one has failed. The medium represents opportunity. It takes creativity to put it into action. But beware of the tendency to become absorbed in the technology rather than the opportunities it offers.

through its print, film, and television holdings. The common denominator, and what Time Warner ultimately says it sells, is entertainment. Its core competency is entertainment. By focusing on this solution, Time Warner is prepared to adopt new technology and add content as it moves forward.

Create Your Tombstone

If you want to start focusing on solutions, start by writing your company's epitaph. In fact, have everyone in the company participate in the project. The natural instinct will be to write about successful products and services for which you wish to be remembered.

Now take out the specific product and service references and focus on the big picture: Perhaps the developer and marketer of detergent-free, all-natural household cleansers becomes "Benevolent employer who protected the environment." And the original purveyor of 24-hour pizza delivery services becomes "Always guaranteed customers the ultimate in convenience." And, finally, the mom-and-pop grocery on the corner is "Neighborhood store with a heart." You get the picture.

Rule 3: Open Yourself to New Ways of Doing Old Business

There's always been more than one way to skin a cat. Each company creates its own technique as it develops. Sometimes your method may even become your niche, as in the case of Norwegian salmon (refer back to Chapter 3, p. 61). The Norwegians not only created a whole category—fresh salmon available anytime anywhere—they defined quality. Yet when the U.S. government put a tariff on the import of whole fish, the Norwegian salmon industry walked away from the market rather than change. While it would have taken some effort, the Norwegians could have reinvented their process, revised their thinking, and converted from shipping what had become a fresh commodity to providing a value-added product. To avoid the tariff, value adding was the answer. In the end, their decision not to change opened the market to other countries. Five years later, Norway has decided to begin the change to value adding now that other countries have paved the way.

As your company grows, you may find yourself needing to develop new ways of doing old business more than once. Tasks that were always performed in-house may become more economical to outsource. You may find financial and strategic reasons to spin off parts of your business as wholly or partially owned subsidiaries. For example, a large institution that provides employees with meal service may decide to create a separate food service business. This might enable the new business to service other companies in the area, which may bring in more revenue or at least offset some of the costs of the service. It could enable you to provide valued employees with new opportunities for vertical advancement. You may have a better chance of keeping a fine up-and-coming young chef who can become vice president of Food Service Inc.

Rule 4: Protect Your Image, Change the Product

Just as you need to focus your business on solutions, you need to protect your image. Image is built on public relations, commitment to quality, word of mouth, and advertising. All too often we want to tinker with our advertising image. Why? Usually because a new director of advertising wants to put his or her stamp on the company. Also because we are much more attuned to our own ad campaigns than our customers are and, accordingly, tire of them more quickly. Our own experience at Holt, Hughes & Stamell is that clients get tired of their message long before it has begun to penetrate the market. For this reason, consider your image changes carefully because each swipe of the new broom whisks away a piece of your image.

Take a few lessons from the marketing giants: "Weekends were made for Michelob" was an effective advertising campaign. Research had shown people were willing to treat themselves on the weekends and pay a little more for their favorite beer. This campaign captured that concept perfectly. Can you remember the current Michelob campaign? On the other hand, several decades after its introduction, who can forget Wisk detergent's "Ring around the Collar" ads. Are you tired of them? Probably not, and they still sell Wisk. Similarly, Philip Morris has not only kept the Marlboro Man but also created a whole line of clothing around the western image.

Rule 5: Look for New Cracks

Even if you have looked in the cracks and found a niche once before, you are not immune to change. All the same forces are still at work. The competition moves in, crowding your once unique position. Or market needs change, forcing you to redefine your business.

For example, same-day cleaning services created a powerful niche in the cleaning business. Today, though, most cleaners can provide same-day

Play a Game of Taboo

Describe your business without using a key word or phrase. For example, describe Disneyland without using the word *theme park*. Describe Amtrak without using the words *rail* or *train*. Describe your own firm without using the name of the product or the words *make, manufacture* or *service*. By forcing yourself to focus outside the box, you will rely on solutions and benefits and image. You might even redefine your mission or find new opportunities in the process.

or next-day service if you ask. But what if you change your emphasis to convenience? Home delivery is one possibility, but that doesn't help if no one is home during the day. A dry cleaner servicing Fairfield County, Connecticut, found a solution: cleaning for commuters. Each weekday morning, customers drop off their laundry and cleaning before boarding the train for Manhattan. They pick up their clean clothes upon returning to the station that same evening. What could be easier?

Well, how about adding other services, such as a piping hot dinner waiting for you at the station? Now the commuter has two chores completed with no more effort than it takes to go to work and come home.

To use a broader example, what happens as the number of home-based workers, telecommuters, and virtual offices increases? What happens to the companies that own and rent office space? Perhaps fewer couriers will be needed to rush packages across town. Delivery businesses based in large metropolitan areas should be worried and busy planning for this prospect. Even if the commuters' exodus is never more than a pipe dream, companies should be doing their contingency planning now. And who should be thinking about the new services that will be needed in suburbs and residential areas if this comes to pass? Suburban teleconferencing centers might be a business for the storefront desktop-publishing centers to consider. Will there be a greater need for suburban couriers to speed a package into the office downtown? Perhaps. And lunch wagons and sandwich delivery services that frequent large construction sites might put residential neighborhoods on their routes. The opportunities are endless.

Outside-the-Box Solution

Speaking of focusing outside the box, did you ever figure out how to connect the nine dots with four lines, as we challenged you on p. 24? Remember, you can't lift your pencil from the page.

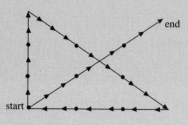

Rule 6: Compete against Yourself

Sooner or later, some combination of sales, research, and personal vision will tell you, "Kill your product. End the service." Conventional wisdom, however, always has been to wait until sales slow to a snail's pace, to try to milk every dollar of R&D invested before introducing the new and improved model. You should plan your own products' obsolescence by competing against yourself. Let's start by dispelling a few myths.

First, introducing a new product rarely kills the older model, although we've heard this a thousand times: Television will kill the movie industry. And when television didn't, then industry insiders feared video would kill movies. Then came: Cable will kill the networks. And so on. Granted, all media industries change with the advent of a new medium. But once the panic dies down and companies adjust to change, they adapt. Today radio programming is music and talk. The radio soap operas moved over to television, where they have a larger audience than ever. Hollywood produces fewer B movies and concentrates on trying to create blockbusters. The made-for-television movie is today's equivalent of the old B movie.

It's even possible for expansion of a category to expand the market. Today there are more people than ever before enjoying entertainment in various forms, not just more varieties of entertainment competing for the same market. Although video sales are up, more people went to the movies last year (1995) than in recent years. The fact is, we have expanded our tastes for media. We do it all—theater, movies, videos, tapes, CDs—often simultaneously. Just watch a teenager trying to do homework with both the radio and television on. The media blitz has made most of us more than accustomed to sensory overload—we like it.

Second, if you don't compete against yourself and come out with new products, your competition surely will. Then you will not only lose sales for your older products, you risk losing your customers altogether. It's better to dig into the products and services that lead customers to your modified watering hole than to have them searching for a fresh drink at your competitor's well. You need to compete against yourself before the customer's cry for "Water! Water!" becomes deafening.

> **If you don't compete against yourself and come out with new products, your competition surely will.**

The government's decision to establish new labeling laws has had an impact on many popular foods. Nabisco's Oreo brand has been one of the best-selling cookie brands for 30 years. Oreos, however, are high in fat content, which the new labels make quite clear to consumers. As a result, this perennial favorite has lost some market share to Nabisco's SnackWell brand, which for the first months after introduction disappeared from shelves almost as fast as they were restocked. Nabisco also gave Oreo a lower-fat alternative, saving the brand from possible extinction. Nabisco has thus positioned itself well, but because they watch trends and remain agile, it hasn't taken other cookie companies long to follow suit. Low-fat cookies now abound on grocery shelves.

To a certain degree, Levi's Dockers compete with the company's blue jean market (see p. 44). But this is no reason to pass over the growing movement toward casual dress clothing—especially when major corporations are allowing their employees to dress down. And if you are a suit manufacturer, you should be working like crazy to establish yourself in this niche with a new line of casual business clothes. If you don't, you risk losing many customers to the likes of Land's End and J. Crew.

Prepare for the Worst

If you are leery of competing against yourself, then map out the possible impact. Create a series of scenarios that outline all the ways you could win and lose by competing against your own products and services, including ways you can best position the old and the new for maximum advantage. For example, you may decide that while the market for your older, low-end product is still strong, in six or eight months the new technology will be the standard. You can choose to beat your competition to market, or follow with the rear echelon. It's your choice. Perhaps you will decide to introduce your new product as the "professional" model with a price to match.

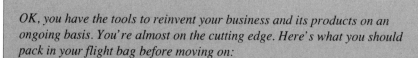

OK, you have the tools to reinvent your business and its products on an ongoing basis. You're almost on the cutting edge. Here's what you should pack in your flight bag before moving on:

- Analyze your successes with the same energy you celebrate your mistakes.
- Ward off extinction by focusing on the future and the changes occurring around you.
- Develop contingency plans.
- Reinvent yourself by transforming, not by evolving.
- Compete against your own products and services before your competition takes up the challenge.

CHAPTER 6

Keep Your Business on the Cutting Edge

"Originality is simply a pair of fresh eyes."
—Thomas Wentworth Higginson

Breakthrough Creativity

The toughest challenge successful entrepreneurs face is keeping their companies on the cutting edge. We've discussed many of the techniques you should apply to this task: institutionalizing risk, viewing failure as a learning process, listening to customers, thinking outside the box, keeping your competition in sight, competing against yourself, and remaining true to your vision. But above all, you need to remain open to new ideas and fresh perspectives.

To help you break out of the handcuffs of past success, we suggest you sharpen your native instincts and create a business plan (a term we use very loosely) to apply creativity to all the tasks we have discussed throughout this book.

Creativity is more than the basis for every new concept, every new company. It is a way of thinking that enables you to solve all the challenges you will face, in business and in all aspects of life. We often confuse "a creative," one who creates art for pleasure or a living, with being creative. In fact, to be creative, you don't have to be a painter, a writer, a master chef, an agency creative—or any of the things we typically attribute to creative professions. Quite simply, creativity is originality. It is finding a new way to do something. "Creativity," says Richard Roth, who has been part of the creative process himself for more than 20 years, "is something I haven't seen before that does the job, that gives new form, effective form, to something that somebody hasn't done before."

> **Quite simply, creativity is originality. It is finding a new way to do something.**

Creativity is the ability to look at natural spring water and say, I can sell that. It's the ability to look at glacial ice in Greenland and say, "Wow, this would make great ice cubes for parties—a real conversation piece." It's also the ability to design an organization that contains a variety of different personalities and opinions throughout—from the mailroom to the boardroom—and have them work together effectively. Creativity is the vision to see new technology as mainstream consumer products. It's the foresight to speculate about the future and make it happen. In short, it's the power to conceive fresh, new ideas that work.

Creativity is a talent we all have if we are willing to open up and apply our thinking to the task. At the same time, we can't impose creativity. We

have to *nurture* our natural creative talent by creating an open, risk-free environment that encourages people to work through roadblocks by questioning and challenging the norm and coming up with solutions. This requires management to encourage people to step back and think about a solution for a few days.

"You can't be the only person who comes up with ideas," says Rory Strunk, himself a creative force in media. "The frustrating part for anyone in business is they get to a point where they're thinking that they're the only person the ideas can come from, because then that company will stagnate at some point." But encouraging creativity requires you to open yourself to people who are willing to challenge the past, in short, those least wedded to the success of the status quo. More often than not, you will find them on the periphery of the business, far from corporate headquarters. Seek out these people and bring them into the creative mainstream of your business.

It's not always easy, admits Michael Stolper, "to vest authority in someone essentially the age of your children or closer to your children's age than your own" because they may not have your experience or knowledge base. But it's essential to keeping the business on the cutting edge. "One of the problems in any corporation" Stolper says, "is it becomes intellectually incestuous, particularly if you are successful. Reluctant to tamper with formulas that have been productive, you become more dismissive of new ideas. You just do what you did yesterday because it worked. That's not to say what we're doing is wrong, but clearly one of the virtues of having younger people around, particularly if they have some presence, is they challenge everything. It's not that they just don't do things the way you did them. They question why you do them this way versus that. I think that's an essential stimulus in any business. [The past] becomes the path of self-destruction when we ritualize the things we did. It's not as though the work doesn't get done, but [the people with new ideas and inquiring minds are] as catalytic as anything else."

In our own offices at Holt, Hughes & Stamell, we're always looking for ways to provide the staff with the tools they need to develop their ideas and stimulate their thinking. One way we encourage creativity is through access to information. For the past several months, we've had a researcher on staff who can find answers to people's work-related questions. This has worked well. But as anyone who has pursued a question knows, sometimes the answer we think we want often leads to another, even better source of information. For this reason, we see value in giving our staff direct access to information via on-line databases so they can explore on their own, with our researcher available to give technical advice as needed.

Mentoring is another tool we are trying to use. Although the process is not formalized, all staff have easy access to senior people. We try to share our experience in an environment that is nurturing and designed to build self-confidence without destroying egos or killing their fresh perspectives and out-of-the-box thinking. We also encourage people to communicate openly and share ideas across departments, such as encouraging an account manager to meet with and help out an intern.

Creativity, when applied to a client's particular need, can even lead to the formation of a strategic alliance. In the case of the State of Maine, we allied with other local talent (our competition under other conditions)

Virtually Creative

When you think of creative force and car dealerships, you naturally think of their promotional talents—the hype—not the process of selling cars. The business, which evolved from the local carriage dealer on the corner, has been fairly straightforward: Find a large piece of land on the outskirts of town, pave it, buy your inventory using a floor-plan loan, and start selling cars. It used to be that customers bought off the showroom floor; those who wanted a lot of options could custom-order their car, which was delivered in a month or two.

But the costs of real estate and borrowing money, coupled with a move toward more standard features and fewer options on cars, may be leading dealers to more creative and cost-effective approaches. An auto mall outside Washington, DC, for example, may represent one creative solution: Sell a dozen or more makes and models of cars under one roof, thus spreading real estate costs among several dealers. Technology may provide the other half of the equation. In the future, just-in-time inventory, CD-ROM, and virtual reality may put you in the driver's seat by simulating much of the auto-buying experience: The dealership may have only a handful of cars in the showroom and a whole parking lot on disk. Want to know how a model performs on the road? Drive the green one in the showroom. Don't like the color? Want a sport package? Sit in the virtual red one with black interior. Opt to put the top down. Select your color and option package, and your car is delivered to a central location within a week.

to create a pool of resources that could serve the varied needs of the Department of Tourism and Business Development.

We stimulate our staff's creative energy in a couple of ways. One, which is particularly out-of-the-box, has been a change in our physical plant: We have recently expanded our office to a second floor. In the process of redesigning the floor space to accommodate a stairwell between the two floors, we opened up the center space and put in a small basketball court. Staff members are free to use this space to blow off steam, build team spirit within the company, or shoot a few baskets while mulling over a creative problem.

We also are using our E-mail system to pose provocative ideas designed to generate on-line conversations that challenge creativity across the staff, inviting everyone to comment and free-associate. The topics have even included a discussion of whether time is linear or cyclical. We have discussed ideas for using the Internet in new and creative ways.

We once posted a surprise art gallery in our kitchen area and asked people to remark about their personal feelings about art and inspiration. One employee responded, "I was really thrown off this morning when I came to work because it was unexpected. My routine was shaken up. People have talked about things differently." Another person wrote, "I enjoyed the pieces [of art] in the kitchen. They made me look. They made me think. They enabled me to start my day on a different note (which I badly needed)."

We have continued to reinforce our creative spirits, both independently and as a group. Recently, for example, we worked together with a well-known maker of handmade paper to learn about the art of handmade paper and the technique for embedding small objects into the paper. Each of us created paper using embedded objects—flowers, locks of hair, shells from a local beach, grass from a favorite field, tickets from a Grateful Dead concert, photos, and other trinkets—that served as our personal expressions. We then took the 35 unique papers and wove them together to create a large wall hanging that resembles a quilt. Not only was the activity fun and creative (some even said spiritual), but we feel the finished work of art represents our company—beautiful and extremely busy.

The on-line, free-form discussions have had the added benefit of allowing us to learn more about ourselves and each other as people. They have helped us appreciate a little more fully the diverse group we represent, with our different likes and dislikes, unique ways of expressing ourselves, and many different sources of pleasure and inspiration.

Sources for Inspiration

In the course of interviewing successful entrepreneurs for this book, we asked them where they found their inspiration. Their answers suggest the range of resources people rely on and may give you ideas for inspiring yourself and others on staff.

• Rory Strunk, founder of the Resorts Sports Network: "I get my ideas in a variety of ways. Definitely reading and being aware, traveling, looking over the media world and kind of recognizing the changes in the marketplace. And then thinking of niches that may address those new opportunities in the future . . . It also comes from brainstorming with friends and going over various ideas . . . A lot of ideas just come from riding, going to the health club, and quiet time."

• Richard Aster, portfolio manager for the Meridian Fund: "I find I'm much more productive and feel like I'm getting a lot more done when I'm listening to companyspeak or when I'm on an airplane just reading, not being bothered. I can really do some good thinking and some good research. Whereas in an office, I am being interrupted and bothered by a lot of different things. So I get a better perspective on business sometimes just getting away from the office and getting out."

• Marshall Smith, founder of Learningsmith stores and the Cybersmith café: "A lot of my thinking and activities are somewhat on an unconscious level. I can be reading about something. I can be visiting another store. Whatever the input, it gets put in there and kind of churns around and comes out at odd moments and odd ways. That's different from the managerial person who's very conscious of what he's doing."

• Julia Child, world-famous cookbook author, television personality, and self-professed home cook: "I'm looking forward to having a little free time to work in the kitchen and to think more . . . If somebody is always giving out and never taking in—well, you have to take in. The great ideas very often are simple. And in the case of my work, you have to know the subject very well. The more background you have, the more creative you can be, because if you think of some idea and it doesn't work out then you have all your background to call on and combine it . . . [The source of great ideas is] most anywhere. I'm eating something and getting an idea from that. Or talking. And then the presentation. If you're a teacher, you have to present ideas in a way that people will understand."

Our conversation with Julia Child was most interesting because she clearly plays down the visionary aspect of creativity. Rather, she equates it more with imagination, receptivity to ideas, and above all hard work.

Authors: How do you come up with new ideas?

Child: I don't think I have any vision at all. I think it's doing what came along . . . Whether it's chicken or beef or fish, you're doing the same kinds of things. So you try and rope them together so people will get that point. But a lot of people are stymied, whether it's by fear or lack of imagination . . . I don't feel so madly creative, although I have my own points of view. I'm not too much swayed by what other people say . . . If you really enjoy what you're doing, you want to do it the way you want. Be like a sponge and take what they offer and put it in your own computer.

Authors: Do you brainstorm, then create a masterpiece?

Child: I once made a delicious fresh strawberry soufflé. It turned out to be the only thing that never turned out well again. The trouble was that the strawberries exuded so much juice that it just didn't work. I did about 28 or 30 experiments on it . . . It was some kind of a meringue with a soufflé in it. Finally I'd worked out getting the juice out of the strawberries and the lightness of the soufflé, but it kept rising too high. It rose so high it went right up through the oven rack . . . It was very funny. Then somebody came up with a simple solution—just use a wider dish, which I did, and that was the solution. Very often it's something so simple you think, Why didn't I think of that?

Authors: Is there anything that could make your creative process easier?

Child: I haven't had the background in science or chemistry which would have been very useful. But after a while, I work out things, mostly doing it by trial and error . . . You have to learn your craft. If you're studying the piano, once you've mastered the scales and the pedals and fingering, then it comes down to whether you are a great player or not.

Six Ways to Break Creativity Blocks

When people are uncomfortable with their own creativity, or fighting a mental block, you can't get results by just ordering them to be creative. The words alone may frighten them. You need tools to help people break out of the box and encourage them not to be creative but to think differently. The following list is a small arsenal of exercises, rituals, and ceremonies designed to court the creative muse that resides deep within your business.

1. *Completely blocked?* There is a technique called *180 degrees* that forces you to find a fresh path to problem solving. You start with a totally new, sometimes ridiculous, premise or challenge, such as, How do you make coach seating more comfortable? Then you try to brainstorm for the opposite result. In this case, you'd ask, How do you make coach seating more uncomfortable? Then you try to create solutions or improvements for the "uncomfortable" qualities. When we ran this exercise, we came up with the idea of making seating more uncomfortable by making passengers wear enormous helmets. But then, by way of making the uncomfortable feature more pleasant, we suggested that the helmets were really virtual reality helmets, which would entertain passengers and take their minds off the cramped leg room. As you can see, this process forces the mind to perform mental gymnastics. In the process of readjusting your thinking by throwing out all the obvious solutions and going in a different direction, you can come up with some innovative ideas.

2. *Too much negative energy?* When you have a problem and a room full of nay-sayers, the first thing to do is list all of the reasons why that problem cannot be solved. Uncover them, get them out in the open, then put them aside. From then on, if somebody raises one of those reasons, it's already been discussed. It's old news and no longer acceptable.

3. *Focused on the bottom line?* Write down the five basic questions related to solving the problem. All of these issues must be related to the product or service or the customer. Forget costs and profitability for the moment. Focus on the real problem at hand. Later, after you have answered the questions and come up with some viable solutions, you can reintroduce the realities of profits and costs.

4. *Too close to the problem?* Sometimes one problem will begin to look like another to a person whose job it is to focus on that part of your business. As a result, our solutions may become formulaic over time. Try switching places with someone in your department who works on another product or service, or with someone in a different department who focuses on another facet of your product or service. This cross-pollination and access to fresh perspectives may introduce a cutting-edge solution.

5. *Too much mental confusion?* Put your mind in a different space—through meditation, physical exertion, or a fresh surrounding. This is where our basketball court comes in handy. Solving problems is not just a physical exercise we perform. It's spiritual and emotional, and sometimes we need a change of pace or space to open up our minds and become receptive to ideas.

6. *Past failures hanging on?* Try performing rituals, such as blowing up your product or burying it or laying an old failure to rest. If you

The Unconventional Solution

In March 1992, all 3,000 employees of Southwest Airlines and Stevens Aviation came together to witness the resolution of a business disagreement. Kurt Herwald, chairman of Stevens, challenged Southwest's chairman Herb Kelleher to an arm-wrestling match to settle, once and for all, claims to the advertising line "Plane Smart." This was a novel and amicable solution to a business problem that might otherwise have been settled in the courts. The resolution? Herwald won the match, then went ahead and allowed Southwest to use the slogan. Both companies gained a tremendous morale boost and great publicity from the 400 newspapers and radio and television stations that reported the event.

At Holt, Hughes & Stamell, we determined the cost of rent at our old office space by challenging the building owner to a game of miniature golf.

think about the Vietnam War for a moment, one of the reasons the country took so long to deal with it was we never laid it to rest. Ritually speaking, we had trouble beginning the healing process until The Wall memorial went up in Washington. Rituals also work when starting something new. If you have a new project, you can jump-start creativity by performing a ceremony to invite the creative muses to join your efforts. This ritual can generate a lot of positive energy.

Just as you don't want to fall into a rut by solving each new problem with old solutions, you don't want to become vested in your new ideas too quickly. An important component of the creative process is to let your "brainstorm babies" stand on their own. Let the ideas flow—many ideas. Get several solutions on the table so you can select the best one, not necessarily the first one or the only one. Even great artists have been known to paint over their canvases when they know they can do better.

Putting It All Together

Once your creative juices are flowing throughout the company, you have to direct them to business challenges large and small. The application can be as specific as creating an environment for a presentation, which we saw our Norwegian clients perform so effectively before a group of Japanese guests. The event was a day-long conference in Oslo to explore the potential for joint business opportunities between the two countries. Rather than provide the typical coffee breaks, during which everyone usually makes a mad dash for the phone, the Norwegians entertained their visitors in the morning with a short piano performance with vocal accompanist. Having concluded a round of morning meetings, the Norwegians introduced the musical interlude by saying, "Well, our discussions have given us something to reflect on as we listen to this." In the afternoon, the Japanese guests reciprocated by performing a traditional tea ceremony.

Seafood entrepreneurs Norman and James Stavis, in Massachusetts, developed a creative means to service the Red Lobster restaurant chain with daily fresh seafood deliveries. Rather than supply the chain through Red Lobster's central distribution, the restaurants use computers to send their orders directly to the Stavises, who then deliver to the individual restaurants the next day using Emory Express services.

We found that our conversations with the entrepreneurs we interviewed for this book not only provided us with inspiration but also uncovered several practical examples of creativity applied under real-world conditions. Given the richness of the conversations, we will let them tell their stories in their own words.

Marshall Smith, creator of Learningsmith, Cybersmith, and other ventures, has been innovative in the way he groups information by category in his stores. He is a risk taker in the sense that much of his research is intuitive and on-the-job. Smith uses a variation of the "compete against yourself" theme by using himself as a model for the customer.

> ***Smith:*** I primarily go about setting up a concept with me as the customer . . . a consumer who is somewhat like me . . . [In the case of the bookstore concept] a lot of stores at that time were primarily gift bookstores. We geared ourselves to people who like to read . . . As for the video stores, I'm interested in the classics, old-time movies, Nova-type things, foreign movies, so the video stores had a much greater emphasis on that part of the industry than a typical video store. So again, I'm kind of a customer, and I choose that niche to go for.
>
> ***Authors:*** How do you target your market?
>
> ***Smith:*** Most of the stores that I have started are aimed high . . . I try to go more to the head, so people think when they come into this store . . . It narrows the market because the market I single out is a

relatively small part of the total market and, to an extent, that limits the competition because the really big guys "market" the total market. We choose a smaller part and hope there will be less competition out there. And it differentiates us.

Authors: What is the source of your innovation?

Smith: I never had a sense of being innovative. To me it has always been logic . . . I see this Cybersmith as a direct extension of the first bookstore . . . I see what I've done not really as innovation or reinvention but as a kind of a logical step in thinking that, for whatever reason, other people haven't done . . .

Authors: How do you channel your creativity into a marketing philosophy?

Smith: I think the idea of the stores is to aim at a defined market and then to create an atmosphere that is welcoming so that a lot of people will come into the store, feel good about being in a store that is somewhat intellectually challenging, but not feel intimidated . . . It's important to have respect for what the customers want and a sense of mission that what we're doing is worthwhile . . .

We did some market research in this store [Cybersmith] and found that people wanted to come in to learn about the Internet, but they wanted to have an enjoyable experience. So the educational part brought them in, but they wanted to make sure they enjoyed themselves while they were there.

Authors: What suggestions would you give to someone just starting a business?

Smith: Stick to what you know . . . In starting a new concept, I would guess every time the first store or the first attempt had more wrong with it than right. But the concept was right . . . If you're willing to make mistakes, and sometimes they can be costly, and if the underlying concept is right, I think you'll be okay after you come through it. You always try to build in some kind of contingency reserve, but too often that contingency reserve is not enough . . . But if you can control it enough, then you're okay.

It was more than a decade ago when Rory Strunk first saw the ski movies his friends were making and showing on the closed-circuit ski channel.

Strunk: I said, boy, there is a versatile marketing plan—a ski magazine, except it's got sight and sound and motion and television going for it. If you could basically duplicate that working model all across the country maybe, if you have enough mass to do it, you might be able to get some national advertisers to buy in. That was the concept nine years ago.

Authors: What kind of reaction did you get when you presented your idea to prospective advertisers?

Strunk: "It sounds good, neat idea," but what I really needed to find were those people who really knew what I was talking about. A man at Audi, for instance, really knew. He had a product that matched the ski market. He had been to enough ski resorts to know that this wasn't a leap of faith that someone, a skier, was going to watch a ski movie. So it caught him.

Authors: What was the prime motivating factor behind your project?

Strunk: Money wasn't my motivator. Maybe the lifestyle was motivating—so I can ski. But the big motivating factor was that no one was doing this . . . If you don't go out to the marketplace and see what's going on, you quickly come up dry. To some extent, it is my lifestyle that I like to do, but part of it is a real legitimate need to know, like snowboarding is creating a huge surge in a whole different general market and a very exciting end of the business that wasn't there five years ago. So if you don't go out there and see that firsthand, you don't know how to address your programming or how to sell to your clients. So I think the point of trying to stay out there as much as possible and make it is the R&D.

Authors: How do you stay focused?

Strunk: Staying true to our mission is a big factor. Our mission is to be the premium media for reaching the top tier of outdoor recreation. And being very innovative and creative in the ways that we are going to attain it—basically building our business and growing it. Whether it's through the Internet, whether it's through other distribution channels. Creativity is a huge part of this. Although clients can come and go every six months, we've kept our clients, probably on average, five or six years. Because we're always on that forefront of creativity. That's actually critical because once it starts to get old, gets to be old hat, then I as a creative person will want to move on and create something different and new. We're nine years into our business, but I feel like it's day one right now because there is so much new opportunity and it's so exciting. It's great for entrepreneurs . . . The tough part is to have the patience to . . . adjust to so many things so fast, but that's where a good management team comes into play. There has to be someone there that reins in a little bit and says, "Hey, we've got to have patience here. Let's wait and see where this goes." That's probably my biggest challenge, having the patience to wait for certain market cues that feel more right than others.

Authors: Is technology driving many of your business decisions?

Strunk: Technology is not entirely the driving force. I'm always out there finding creative ways to move our product in cheaper, more-efficient ways to the benefit of our clients in order to get more reach, to get a bigger audience . . . That can be done by better programming, good quality programming . . . so a big part of it is the content. The content is somewhat removed from everything that's happening so fast out there in the marketplace, so there is a very strong focus on content in our business. We look to the technologies to milk them for all they're worth.

Authors: It must have been a big risk for you to jump from cable to the Internet.

Strunk: When we started the Internet project, it was a big upheaval in our company because it was so different. It was change, and change is scary to a lot of people. We had to bring people along in our office and say, "This is good because it's going to establish our brand-new change. We want to do this and this and this." But deep down everybody is wondering, "Is this going to eclipse our core business?" We don't know that right now . . . The marketplace will decide what is going to last and what isn't going to last. I would say that that's one of the reasons why we go out and do these new things because if our core business is going to be outdated at some point in the future, we'd better have a fallback position and we'd better be on the edge of that new media. Around the country—be it newspaper companies, telephone and cable companies—all are seriously looking at their product and going forward . . . The people who aren't doing that are running a futuristic failure.

Authors: How do you adapt to a rapidly changing marketplace?

Strunk: The changes happening in technology are happening so fast that you can't [let yourself] be blinded . . . If you think they're going to change five years from now, chances are you'd better cut that in half because it will happen, probably faster than you think it will. But really what you've got to do is look at your product, and you've got to look at the marketplace for some change. You've got to look at demographic change . . . We have to prepare for an aging U.S. audience . . . Virtually every company has to look into that type of marketplace and review it constantly."

The Internet, of course, is spawning considerable interest these days. This and other on-line communication systems represent a real frontier of opportunity, with potential to revolutionize not only communications but also retailing, advertising, distribution, and more. Both Marshall Smith and Rory Strunk have made their initial plunges into this rich arena and are looking for ways to keep their growth and future efforts on the edge of technological and sociocultural developments.

In the following interview excerpt, Smith tells of starting Cybersmith.

> *Smith:* I was interested in the Internet and asked my kids what it was. They told me they were both on the Internet and told me four or five times, but I still didn't look at it. Finally I said, "Show me." I sat down at a computer and got it. You have to do it. So where do you do it? There isn't anyplace. That was literally step by step. I was the customer, I had this need, I looked around. Everybody else had the same need; 95 percent of computer owners want to know what the Internet can do and [yet they] don't get it. In answer to the question about will it become extinct, I have to say that if you're tying the store only to the Internet, the answer is probably.
>
> *Authors:* OK, you are predicting the obsolescence of what you do. Right?
>
> *Smith:* But I think the concept is more about new technology, with the Internet being one of those unique things that is overwhelming the world. Videoconferencing is a fascinating area. It's too expensive for people to have in their own home, but we could put it in the store. What's coming next? Who knows what's coming next. We found in our market research that a large number of the people who come in are on-line. So we're dealing with a knowledgeable population who's looking to broaden their knowledge. As long as we have ways to broaden the knowledge of people on the Internet, I think we have an entrenchment . . . with the Internet as the prime moving force. But [we'll expand into] whatever is out there that for

some reason isn't into people's homes yet. We put it in the store first, and in that sense we'll be the introducers . . . I think the main competition will be the Disneys, Warner Brothers, or Blockbusters, where they will have 20 virtual reality experiences but they will also have some of these other things too. Theirs will be a game atmosphere where you can do these other things; we're kind of differentiating ourselves into more of a learning that's fun.

Authors: How quickly do you anticipate change to hit retailers like you?

Smith: The changes will happen in a shorter time frame, and we've got to be much closer to what's happening at the producer's side, at the innovative side in manufacturing or design of products that are coming out . . .

I think I'll always be the customer. Ultimately what will happen is that I will learn the industry as the general public is learning the industry, so I'll be keeping up and maybe a little bit ahead of where the general public is, and I'll always be asking the questions that the general public is asking. But the general public in this area is getting smarter all the time, or at least that part of the public that's younger.

Rory Strunk is striving to create cutting-edge content in this on-line environment: "When you're on the edge and you're doing new things, you're always going to be a step ahead of a certain group out there . . . You don't have to be one of the Time Warners of the world to have a good product on the Internet. Distribution is an equal opportunity for everyone. So you take that model and say, 'Everybody has an equal shot at the same distribution. What is going to filter out as the most successful factor? Is it going to go down to viewership and your ability to drive viewership? Is it going to be based on quality content?' That's where Time Warner definitely has an edge; because they have resources, they really can do it right. But entrepreneurs can dig down and come up with good quality content without the same resources, so I would say the content is going to be more and more important in the future as the media world gets more and more fragmented with people looking for more programming that's special . . . That, I think, bodes well for our future . . . You can be out there and you can control your own distribution, and you're not playing by anybody's rules." Strunk adds: "Everybody's looking at the Walt Disney content, and they are incredible at extending the value chain of their products. If you look at 'Beauty and the Beast' there are a million different ways they promote the product."

Like Smith's and Strunk's, your challenge is to apply your native creativity to the ways you do business—through promotion, organization, product design, niche development, controlling costs, and so on. To work through these issues, you need a plan. Let's explore the options.

Facilitating Your Creativity

To bring your creative efforts to fruition and save them from being mere creative meanderings, you need to devise an organizational model that at the very least suggests a general direction for your thinking and helps channel your growth. Your plan or model should help galvanize the company without imposing a strict timetable or structure.

In achieving success, the emphasis should be on realizing your vision. Without the visionary part, you are merely reacting to events. You want an order that stimulates your ability to be proactive. A vision helps you express the culture or context within which change and growth are facilitated. Without a vision for the big picture, you will never understand what is currently driving your business decisions. And you won't know when to break away to something new. Without that visionary understanding, you will be doomed to change the things that only *appear* wrong or appear not to be central to your organization without ever really knowing you are doing the right thing. So, while you need some sort of organization, the plan itself is always secondary to the vision.

There is no right or wrong way to structure your creativity and, ultimately, your success. The structure is little more than an acknowledgment of your business potential. This is the real reason we even advocate a formal plan of some sort. It comes down to doing what works and feels right to you. As Rory Strunk explains: "We often go into things knowing that we aren't going to make money for a while, and we project them that way. We look for that trend to switch when we predicted it would switch. So we definitely use timetables to kind of gauge our success or evaluate it . . . I'll ultimately feel like it [the sports network] has become successful when it achieves the total vision of what we want to accomplish and we [have become] . . . a very creative and dynamic company."

The fact that some entrepreneurs feel more comfortable following their gut—they do something, they make mistakes, they learn, and they go on—should not preclude them from creating some form of structure.

Think Futures; Act Now

This is an exercise you can perform as a group. Create a companywide conference of the future, your future. Ask people on staff to present on various topics of future gazing—technology, environment, customer expectations, competition, and so on. You might even arrange for a guest speaker to kick off your event and provide some general perspectives on what the future may hold. Follow the discussions and presentations with a group exercise to determine what kinds of effects these changes might have on your business. Perhaps you will manufacture in outer space where weightlessness will be an advantage. Perhaps you will see competition coming from a new source. Ask yourselves, "Why will we still be able to compete?"

You could formalize the activity by creating a corporate white paper based on the results. Treat the event as an opportunity to break out of the box, but don't formalize it into a 10-year or 20-year plan. Rather, focus on the general capabilities the company has to adapt to the future. These quite probably are the core competencies that will help you succeed in the next few years as well—only the specific applications will differ. If you like the direction you see, build on these capabilities. If you don't, start trying to build new capabilities into the business—capabilities that will give you the flexibility to adapt when the future arrives.

For times when they need a road map that provides step-by-step progression, the plans should be for the short term and should heavily reflect specific objectives.

The difficulty is knowing how to create a structure that gives direction while maintaining flexibility. One way is to create different types of plans for different time frames. The shorter the time period, the more specific you can be. The longer the time, the more general you need to be. For example, we conducted an exercise for a client in the seafood business and asked the company's representatives to think about their industry in the 21st century. Their natural instinct was to say, "OK, what will it be like in the year 2000? But that's less than five years away." We said, "Forget about that. What will it be like in the year 2030?" By trying to imagine your business 35 or 40 years out, you instinctively know that you can't possibly imagine all the factors that will have impact—technology, competition, environmental issues, and so on. The exercise forced

Leave the Details to Those Closest to the Action

Häagen-Dazs International has a Director of Magic whose job it is to encourage the people closest to the business (store managers and counter people) to be creative and voice their ideas. If the company's mission—Dedicated to Pleasure—is going to work, managers believe, it needs to be present in every store. Every trip to the ice cream store needs to be an enticing pleasure, and only the people working in the stores can create this environment.

them to stop building on the existing platform for the moment and thus freed their imagination and creativity.

Think of your plan as a living document that not only reflects the collective vision of people in the company but also can be adapted to a wide range of time frames. Without limiting opportunity, it can establish limits of where you don't want to go. Think of a plan as a series of doors to get you out of the box of conventionality. It is not a blueprint or road map. That level of detail should be left for planning the immediate future—say the next 100 days or six months at most—and should include specific input from individual departments and smaller groups that work together on the project level. What will keep them on track, however, is a general direction, the big picture or vision for the company. This kind of collaboration increases companywide buy-in and encourages everyone to take ownership.

> Think of your plan as a living document that not only reflects the collective vision of people in the company but also can be adapted to a wide range of time frames.

To further facilitate creativity, companies should focus on their core competency. Fortune Sails, for example, is a sailmaker, but the company's core competency is to stitch fabric together in any shape and reinforce it to withstand intense pressure. With this understanding, Fortune has been able to move beyond making sails to making covers for radar and radio telescopes, which today is a bigger part of its business than sailmaking because the company focused on its skill rather than on a particular product.

Plan Builders

To help you move away from creating the conventional two-year plan or five-year plan, we have devised a couple of exercises to help you focus on core elements of the business and vision. You will gain the creative freedom to apply your core competencies, as they often are called, in any number of ways.

1. *Create a business plan without numbers.* In other words, don't focus your plan on cost and profit projections. That level of detail comes later and for specific projects. Your plan should be general enough to allow for several extensions or developments to be running in parallel.

2. *Create a vision statement without nouns.* Use only verbs. For example, a shoe company sews. A retailer sells or provides. An agency services. Focusing on verbs allows you to see the broad capabilities, not narrow product or service offerings. Had ice companies of the late 19th century, for example, focused on the verbs *refrigerated* or *shipped,* rather than on the product—ice—they might have more easily made the transition into artificial refrigeration. Similarly, if you make fax machines, your verbs are *duplicate, transmit, communicate,* and *make.* You fall into a trap when you start defining business in terms of the specific products and services you provide. Our method helps you focus on opportunities for creating new businesses or reinventing a new one within your present structure.

As you can see, it's a technique any organization can use. For example, state and municipal governments should look at their bond offerings this way because if a flat tax structure is adopted, this form of financing construction and maintenance of infrastructure may be less inviting to investors seeking tax-free income. Rather, their business is financing. With the focus off bonds, they are freer to create competitive new investment opportunities for the future. In the same way, accountants need to identify their core capa-

Honda has taken much the same approach. Management did not see the company as a motorcycle manufacturer but rather as a group of engineers who specialize in engine design. As a result, Honda has been able to see itself clear to put its engines into any number of machines ranging from automobiles to lawnmowers.

Even a service provider, such as an advertising and marketing agency, can use this approach. An agency that "communicates" can be an advertising and public relations firm, a developer of direct-mail campaigns, a creator of integrated marketing and communications strategies, a newsletter and CD publisher/producer, a communications services provider, a software developer, and much more. Any combination is possible—provided, of course, the company has the requisite skills.

Too much planning can, in fact, leave you standing still. The following is an experiance that taught a lesson in overplanning. As part of a training exercise used by the Outward Bound program on Hurricane Island in Maine, 20 people are directed to enter a cave where the rock formation provides a path no wider than one person. Suddenly the group comes to a dead end. The only way out is to climb up to a crack above them and go through it to the other side. As part of the exercise, the people are lined up alternating a big or tall person with a small or short person. They are instructed to climb up and exit the cave through the crack in exactly this order. They have 20 minutes to do it. The group members argue for 19 minutes about how to solve the problem. Then a warning call comes down that they only have one minute left. They stop planning and rely on brute force and determination as they claw their way through the crack. Somehow everyone manages to squeeze through the crack in less than a minute. The moral of the exercise is that sometimes you have to abandon formal planning and just do it.

The Outward Bound people report that the pattern is the same every time. People argue about the right solution, then when pressed for time they just do it. And in every case, everyone gets through just under the 20-minute time limit. Now think of the business opportunities you have waiting for you on the other side of your obstacles. Too often we hold back. If you rely only on your plans, you may never break out and test your ability to work past obstacles. Remember, we are limited only by the knowledge and ideas we have at any one time. We don't know if we can slip through the crack until we try. Sometimes you just have to do it. Consider your plans to be part of the exercise, not a diagram for getting through the crack.

The further danger of too much planning is that you will never reinvent your company, you will only evolve according to past successes.

The further danger of too much planning is that you will never reinvent your company, you will only evolve according to past successes. The fact is, unleashing creativity requires you to take an occasional leap of faith. Business should not follow nature's plan. You don't have to exist as a caterpillar before you can be a beautiful butterfly—not if you have the creativity and core competencies to take off now. There is always the danger that if you sink all your capital and thinking into being a caterpillar first, you may remain a caterpillar forever.

Prepare yourself to move not only swiftly but decisively. As we've said before, one of the easiest ways to do this is to assume everything you have done in the past failed. When you see an opportunity, put your plans aside and develop a new paradigm. The U.S. auto industry faces such a dilemma today, even in the face of their successes over the past couple of years. Although Detroit has made a strong recovery, carmakers are still thinking like caterpillars.

Through the Partnership for a New Generation of Vehicles, the Big Three automakers have taken up the government's challenge to collaborate to create a car by the year 2000 with triple the efficiency of today's models. But the fact is, new technology coupled with creative thinking could enable the automakers to make a quantum leap. If only they could throw out all the old blueprints and rethink the automobile from the concept up. If they left the traditional steel carriage behind and applied new plastics and aerodynamics, they could create long-range machines with not 3 but 8 to 10 times the fuel efficiency of today's cars.

The radical new car of the future would be more chips and plastic than steel and fuel efficiency. It is a car so radically different, it is actually possible that Silicon Valley might be the more logical source of inspiration than Detroit.

The issue is not whether to have a plan but rather how to develop a process that works for you, one that gets you thinking and enables you to keep moving forward rather than stagnating. You can't sit back comfortably with a 20-year plan and execute mindlessly. And if you think you can't move forward without a 20-year plan, then create a new one every year.

With your creativity stimulated, no doubt you are anxious to get going. But before you journey on, place these ideas in your flight bag:

- Everyone is capable of being creative.
- Have fun and follow your instincts.

CHAPTER 7

Can We Talk?

"To live, to err, to fall, to triumph, to create life out of life."
—James Joyce

The Well-Integrated Organization

It's long been said that if you build a better mousetrap, the world will beat a path to your door. That's an old adage we'd like to dispel. Delivering new products alone is not the answer. You can't operate on the assumption that all you have to do is engineer the perfect product solution, and the rest becomes a marketing and sales problem. All too often marketing departments and outside agencies are called in after a product is developed and left with the challenge of figuring out how to add value and build in margin. If you are an engineer, you start with product. If you are a marketer, you start by leveraging your distribution system and your old network.

Some 30 or 40 years ago, with less competition and lower customer expectations, companies could tackle the process in a more linear fashion. They could develop a product, set a price, create a promotion, and push out the product on an unsuspecting and less-sophisticated market. That was then.

This is now: The business process no longer moves conveyor-belt fashion through perfectly articulated and completely separate stages of conceiving, building, promoting, and selling. To succeed, a business must create a living, breathing, organic, and completely relational process that enables management—indeed all employees—to look at every component of the process at the same time. Today, customer, cost, convenience, and communication must be part and parcel of the same conversation; a conversation that begins on day one.

Such an integrated approach to marketing ensures that all communications "speak" in a single, companywide voice; that databases store knowledge of customer purchasing habits that can be applied to subsequent sales campaigns; and that marketing efforts are tracked through to completion of the sales cycle and evaluated for their effectiveness. Similarly, integrated management is about creating an environment for two-way dialogue—talking *and* listening—across the whole company. The consequence of creating more open lines of communication is that the development of products and services—in all their aspects—becomes a companywide responsibility.

But first let's look at a hypothetical example that illustrates what a complete lack of communication and coordination can do to a company bound by tradition and conventionality: A reputable old company has been making pocket calendars for years—fine, leather-bound calendars

"I'm sending you an E-mail in response."

for male executives that fit neatly in a jacket breast pocket. Over the years, the company has been very successful, but that's begun to change.

The sales force is still out there doing the best it can to sell pocket calendars to retailers across the country. It turns out, however, that what the salespeople have learned by talking with their customers—the store owners—is that the market has changed. Fewer people want the traditional black alligator pocket calendar—the company's premier product.

Women want buttery-soft suede organizers in a variety of pastel colors. And they would love it if their organizer could double as a checkbook and change purse when they are out on business. More men than ever before are interested in carrying snappy little electronic personal organizers that can store 3,000 names, phone numbers, and addresses; keep their calendar through the year 2020; and send and receive brief faxes. Furthermore, the sales force has discovered a new, as yet untapped, customer—kids. They want organizers that fit into their school notebooks. And they want them in bright colors with radical graphics and built-in electronic calculators.

The salespeople bring this anecdotal information back to company headquarters, but they fail to deliver a unified message from the field that the product line could benefit from some changes. As a result, no one in marketing or management is prompted to research this apparent market shift, let alone to see what the competition is doing.

To further offset the rumblings coming from the sales force, the crusty old lead designer, who has been with the company for 35 years, says he's added a rich brown ostrich-skin calendar sized especially for women to carry in their purses. "Great," says the president, who hasn't heard any of the stories emanating from the field. "We can make both products without any costly retooling of our operations." To the sales force he says, "This is what we make. Now you go out and sell it. After all, fine calendars are what we have made for more than 75 years. They built this business. We're even giving you a special new product for women. If you can't convince women that black alligator is chic, then sell them on brown ostrich."

But sales continue to fall, which prompts management to ask, "Why can't you sell what we make? Perhaps we should find a new vice president of sales and marketing and send some of the sales force packing at the same time." We have to wonder, Is anyone listening to anyone else in this company?

Maybe this example sounds too extreme. You want to ask, "Who would run their company that way?" Well, it's done every day, and it reflects a polarization between management and other departments. Consider the story of a major New England insurance company that learned its lesson the hard way. The company had built a successful business selling group health plans and compensation packages to companies, when it decided it needed to create a medical insurance product for individuals. The sales force was elated. They knew they could sell such a product and went about doing a little market research on their own. They contacted customers for interviews, looked at what some of the competition was doing, and reported back to headquarters with their findings. In the meantime, management had gone ahead and created its product. But because the managers had worked in a vacuum—without customer, competition, or sales feedback—they produced a product that was twice as expensive as its nearest competitor. With customers shopping more competitively than ever before, how much do you think they sold? Yes, the product failed miserably.

Then take, for example, Uncle Capt'n Vergil's Fresh Frozen Pogie Pies, a company we fabricated from dozens of situations we have witnessed in companies over the years. Uncle Capt'n Vergil's goes to great lengths to create a corporate mission. "Uncle," as everyone calls the CEO, and his top management spent weeks talking among themselves, writing and rewriting their mission: "To produce the finest pogie pie in its price class." It's a message any company would be proud to print in its annual report. The problem, however, has been in implementation. No one at the top thought to integrate the mission into the criteria by which employees are measured.

Every office and manufacturing facility around the country has a huge banner proclaiming the mission. But listen to the conversations at any of the dozen field offices and you will hear a different message. Monday morning the manager says, "We've received a product shipment from the Southeastern plant that is twice the size of last quarter's. So, boys and girls, you've got to go out and sell like hell. I don't want to see a single box of pogie pies in here in three months' time." Like most salespeople, those at Uncle Capt'n Vergil's are being judged on their ability to deliver volume and meet quotas, rather than for upholding the words of the mission and delivering "the finest pogie pie in its price class." There's no integration here.

The point is that while sales leads to the bottom line in this, as in any business, that goal must be accomplished in a manner that is in keeping with the company mission or, as we prefer, vision. Salespeople at Uncle Capt'n Vergil's should feel that they are not selling, rather they are carrying forward the company's objectives to deliver quality and value to all. If they are reduced to liquidating inventory, their measurements do not reflect the vision, and "Uncle" is left wondering why his new message of dedication to quality and value isn't having a greater effect on the bottom line. We could tell him where the problem lies.

Integration also means ensuring that everyone on staff is working for you, not against you, even inadvertently. Take, for example, the story of the local business leader who came to our office one day to discuss his marketing strategy. We spoke for some time before he relaxed and confided he was a little intimidated at the thought of calling an agency like ours with numerous national and international accounts. He was, in his words, only the head of a local business. He said he appreciated the time we spent talking and the quality of the advice we provided. We replied that the size of his account should generate interest from any number of local agencies and recommended that he let them compete for his business. What he said next surprised us.

"I called another agency," he said, "but I couldn't get past the receptionist. She kept asking me for the specific reason for my call. I didn't want to go into detail with her. I just wanted to leave a message for the head of the agency to give me a call." The receptionist warned the businessman that the agency head might not call back unless he knew the exact nature of the call. We had to wonder about her performance review and on what she thought she was being evaluated. Apparently she was an excellent gatekeeper, but what correlation that could have to the agency's vision is a mystery. Clearly this was a case of poor integration and mixed messages, since we sincerely doubt this agency is as elitist or cynical as the receptionist's efforts to guard the palace and protect the boss make it appear.

We all know it pays to talk to as many people as possible—inside the company and out. But at Macro-Micro Digital Works (another hypothetical company created out of our collective experiences) the company's marketing people refused to speak with advertising space reps (salespeople for magazines and air time). Space reps are insiders to the publications and networks and have valuable information about upcoming editorial calendars and programming. By failing to integrate these outside resources into its planning, Macro-Micro Digital Works was losing a chance to hear about stories and upcoming editorial themes that might have fit nicely with the company's public relations objectives. In protecting their time by deflecting all calls to their agencies, the marketing people lost the opportunity to pitch their products directly to the editorial departments.

In another example, recently we were approached by an entrepreneur with a clever concept. He came to us with his product and said, "I want the Olympics to use my product, and I want L. L. Bean to sell it in its catalog. You have connections to both organizations. Will you help me?" By failing to create an integrated strategy for his product, this entrepreneur had made his first fatal mistake. We tried to help by suggesting that he backtrack a little and begin by building momentum for the product and creating market share and interest via an infomercial or one of the home-shopping networks. But he ignored our recommendations, convinced that once he had the product, it was a natural step to gaining worldwide distribution and exposure. So far, this has not happened.

To be effective, the integrated approach must be reflected in a company's strategy. Yet we've actually had clients pull the strategy page out of their communications plans, saying, "I'm glad you understand it and did this, but our people don't need to understand this." Wrong response. The failure to create an integrated strategy can lead a company to adopt tactics that will go nowhere. We know of a microbrewer, for example, that had just one goal—to be acquired by a major beer company. The brewer knew what it wanted but never articulated a strategy for achieving that vision. It had but one plan of action: Erect giant billboards proclaiming its beer in the hopes that this would entice a beer company to buy the company out. This was a tactic, not a strategy.

Another company, a manufacturer of industrial fabrics that branched effectively into the office furniture systems business was recently faced with changes in the industry coupled with increased competition. The company's first thought was to cut prices and pass the savings on to the customer. Unsure what to do, the board turned to outside help and brought in marketing consultants. After much discussion, these "outsiders" created a strategy to integrate the needs of the manufacturer with its suppliers through stronger relationships. The manufacturer hosted an internal conference at which employees determined how they could streamline the business and create integrated new systems from which everyone could benefit. In the end, however, the board threw out the strategy, fired the president, and dumped the consultants. The company had literally come to the edge and had a viable strategy worked out—but then stopped, turned around, and went back to business as usual.

There are dozens of variations on this failure-to-integrate theme, and all come down to four things:

1. Too much reliance on past success.
2. Misunderstanding of organizational dynamics.
3. Poor communication.
4. A vision sent down from the top that receives little or no staff buy-in.

We've discussed the dangers of being blinded by the past, but what about being blinded by organizational dynamics? And why do so many companies have trouble liberating their channels of communication? Much of the problem lies in management's mistrust of employee motives and a firm belief in the hierarchical approach to labor relations—a notion dating from the Middle Ages. Let's look at some common myths in business.

Myth: Most salespeople take the path of least resistance. They sell only what's easy to sell, unless management dangles a carrot in the form of higher compensation on harder-to-sell items.

Fact: It may be human nature to travel the course of least resistance, but what if the resistance is real? Maybe your salespeople are tired of banging their heads against a wall of customer resistance. Maybe there are real reasons your products aren't selling. This is a matter for discussion and honest soul searching on both sides. Management needs to create a safe environment that is free of finger-pointing if it is going to get to the bottom of this problem.

> **Management needs to create a safe environment that is free of finger-pointing if it is going to get to the bottom of this problem.**

Myth: Salespeople always think the grass is greener in some other sector of the market. They are good at turning molehills into mountains. All they ever say is, "If we had a newer model or a different color, we could sell a million." We can't keep retooling our operations based on the whims of the sales force. That's a race we cannot win.

Fact: Salespeople, like most of us, may have a tendency to take a handful of anecdotes and extrapolate them into an avalanche of consumer interest. But the fact remains that these people are closest to your sales. They know if the competition is winning away customers with newer models, colors, and styles. It's up to management to (1) make salespeople quantify their field experiences and (2) follow up with customer and competitive research to determine if they are being beaten out repeatedly by better or more appealing products and services.

Myth: Management likes to play accounting games with us in order to boost sales. They expect us, for example, to sell upscale products to the consumers or retailers of our more moderately priced products. They tell us we're in business to service our clients' needs, but they tie our sales goals to our ability to move boxes out of the warehouse.

Fact: Obviously, any company would like to see its customers trade up. And they're probably right; opportunities of this sort do exist. At the same time, very few CEOs would risk alienating the entire marketplace to make a few extra sales. What management is not hearing from the field are enough real numbers and real stories about what the customer wants. It's time for management to get out in the field more and talk with customers and to shop the competition. It's also time for sales departments to provide their management with a clear, comprehensive picture of their marketplace.

Myth: The staff thinks we are a limitless resource of jobs, opportunity, and money. They don't pay the bills; they just spend our money on extraneous market research, manufacturing goof-ups and long lunch breaks. They take to heart the belief that 99 percent of success is just showing up. Don't they know how hard we work to keep this company together?

Fact: When employees fail to act like owners, it's probably because they don't know what's really going on. They haven't seen a balance sheet, and most have little or no contact with customers. If you want employees to take greater responsibility for their actions, they need to know more about the day-to-day operations of running the business. They need a management that talks with them, not *at* them.

Clearly, companies need to develop a meaningful two-way discourse designed to help management, staff, and sales establish some common ground of understanding that realistically reflects both the company's core competencies and the marketplace. Anything less will reduce a company to a modern-day Tower of Babel, leaving everyone skeptical and pointing fingers at their fellow workers. The sad part is that the components of two-way conversation are so close at hand. The typical company has a great diversity of thought, skills, experience and knowledge. It has accountants, salespeople, manufacturers, marketers, operations experts, and managers. It has senior people with years of on-the-job experience as well as new employees, still wet behind the ears but teaming with fresh perspectives and untested ideas. Together, these people represent a diversity of opinions, ideas, and experience just waiting to fuel a company's growth.

It comes down to drawing these differences out and promoting them—encouraging new employees and younger staff to express their views while providing everyone access to the experience and talents of the most seasoned senior executives. It's there; you just have to nurture it and integrate it into the business's mainstream discussion.

As usual, it's up to management to take the first step toward opening up the lines of communication. Think of the problem as two camps—management and everyone else—ensconced behind their respective fences. Your job is to tear down the fences and get the two sides to come together as one company. The first step, if you want employees to take their jobs as seriously as you do, is to give them a larger view of the picture. The challenge is knowing what's enough and what's too much. How do you balance optimism about the company's future with caution? Our rule of thumb is that the less information you share, the less likely employees are to exhibit the same level of care and concern as owners. You can expect that if you share only good news—the wins—with employees and insulate them from the day-to-day issues of running the business, they will feel complacent and more carefree. In short, they will view their company as a candy store—a place that provides them equipment when they request it and increasing job opportunities as a natural progression. You need to give employees the information that will help them feel like owners so they will take interest and care in everything they do; this includes sharing financial information.

It really comes down to honesty. Management needs to provide an honest reporting of everything that transpires—good and bad. They also need to put the information in context and help employees learn how to interpret what they hear. Every loss should not send them into panic any more than a win is a message that they can kick back and relax. They need to realize that a succession of bad decisions can lead to people being laid off, without fearing for the immediacy of their job. Management, therefore, needs to meet with employees to discuss the overall progress and direction of the business, rather than just list a series of positive events or bad stories after the fact. By sharing in the discussions, all employees will come away with a better understanding of opportunities and gradually even take ownership of the decisions that will turn opportunity into winning strategies. They will develop a sense that every employee shares the responsibility to ensure the company's success.

We realize that this is a difficult step for most executives to take. It's long been the theory that it is easier to get employees to do what management wants when employees don't understand anything beyond their own jobs. In fact, the opposite is true. Without integration, information will flow one way, from the top down, leaving employees with almost no chance to get their messages heard. As a result, employees will retain their candy-store mentality, and the sales force will sell only that portion of the product line their traditional sales channels can handle. And another once-successful company will stall. Only through integration will all employees develop the sense of responsibility, accountability, and understanding that makes a business thrive.

> It's long been the theory that it is easier to get employees to do what management wants when employees don't understand anything beyond their own jobs. In fact, the opposite is true.

This section describes five tactics we at Holt, Hughes & Stamell have developed—as "recovering Pollyannas" ourselves—to address the problems of complacency inside our own company. We think they might be equally valuable for you. As you read each tactic, you'll come to understand the organic nature of our efforts to change. None of these tactics can occur in a vacuum; all are linked and are representative of a larger, systemic revision in the way we run our business. We readily admit that we remain recovering Pollyannas in training. We've made our share of mistakes and have yet to perfect any of these efforts. At the same time, as part of our celebrating the recognition of our mistakes, we continue to try. And the more we try, the more each tactic becomes second nature. We recommend the effort to you.

1. Change Your Management Style

In most firms, management gives instructions and orders, while everyone else takes notes. Traditionally, there is a lot of nodding of heads, little thinking, and very little challenge to the status quo. You can begin to change this with something as simple as the way you present issues. Start, for example, by saying, "I've got this problem; what's your recommendation? How do you think we should handle this? Why don't you go think about this and get back to me tomorrow." For management, it's the difference between being a facilitator and a dictator. In the case of your top creative people, it's the difference between allowing them to be writers and designers versus glorified scribes and mechanical artists. Middle managers have an opportunity to participate in the decision making, rather than merely carrying out the boss's decisions.

2. Introduce Mentoring

The mentoring issue is very closely linked to that of management style. It's mentoring by asking. Again, rather than telling people what to do, ask for their recommendations, then come together to brainstorm. This way, junior people have the benefit of learning from those more experienced in an environment that is positive and nurturing.

3. Commit to Research and Development

Since, in the case of our own agency, our goal is to have at least one if not two new products we can sell within six months, we need to treat research and development (R&D) as a real part of our jobs. We take the lead from British social critic, author, and business consultant Charles Handy, who says senior executives should spend 20 percent of their time in R&D. We all talk R&D, but if it's not in our job descriptions, we never get around to walking the talk. R&D gets short shrift. Making it happen requires building R&D time into our weekly schedules.

4. Hire to Where You Want to Be, Not Where You Are Now

The corollary to this is "spend money to where you want to be, not to where you are now" or, more colloquially, "It takes money to make money." That's how you grow. So now when we hire, we try to determine whether or not the potential employee can think strategically and conceptually, and what his or her ability is to grow in that vein. Let's say, for example, that we hope to expand our computer capability to include the creation of CD-ROM products but that our current needs are more basic—to get everyone up and running effectively on our network. Ideally, we would like to hire a young programmer who can carry us forward into software development while handling our current systems and training needs and creating any custom systems we need today.

5. Reexamine your Growth Strategy and How It Relates to Employees

Managing your growth—not only its rate but also the objectives—requires the right mix of employees and a close evaluation of both your goals and your current staff capabilities and personalities. As you adjust to fill staffing gaps, you must create that delicate balance and take care not to push people forward too quickly. To avoid workforce inflation (a form of grade inflation), companies also need to be honest in the review process, while helping people through education and mentoring. And if you decide to send employees off for training, either professional or personal, make sure they understand exactly why they are being sent.

Under the watchful eye of CEO Jim Shaffer, Guy Gannett Communications has been going through a massive reinvention and repositioning with respect to changes in the media industry. We asked him about his efforts to create an integrated environment in these changing times. "You have to get closer to your people, which in itself is a plus," he says. "You also have to have a supervisory apparatus that isn't hidebound and protective of their own way of doing things . . . I can tell that a lot of people around here turned off to innovation years ago because every time they suggested something they were basically told to sit down, shut up, or worse. We're going to have to be willing to trim off supervisors who are wedded to protecting the way they're doing things. But this is a problem because traditionally top management planned, people at the bottom executed, and the people in the middle kept things stable. Middle management's role wasn't to be visionary, it was to keep things running smoothly as top management tried to impose new programs . . . Now we're trying to change things so fast, the stabilizing force becomes dysfunctional . . . I find it easier to introduce, discuss, and implement these concepts at the lower ranks and the very top ranks than the middle ranks. So we're focusing much of our training on middle management."

Shaffer puts a lot of stock in the quality of the organizational culture. So much so, he assesses employee performance on two axes—cultural and numbers—much the way General Electric's CEO Jack Welch does. All performance falls into one of four quadrants along these axes: low culture, low numbers; high culture, low numbers; low culture, high numbers; and high culture, high numbers. To have a future in the company, employees must score high on their ability either to enrich the working environment (culture) or to deliver business (numbers). A dictatorial

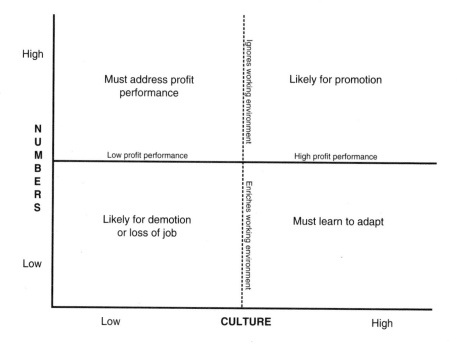

High

**N
U
M
B
E
R
S**

Low

Must address profit
performance

Likely for promotion

Low profit performance

High profit performance

Ignores working environment

Enriches working environment

Likely for demotion
or loss of job

Must learn to adapt

Low   **CULTURE**   High

manager who can't deliver business is history. Those who score high both in culture and numbers are the stars and will be among the first to grow with the company. Everyone else, Shaffer feels, deserves a chance to learn how to improve their ability either to perform within the new company culture or to deliver on the numbers, and the goal is to transform as many employees as possible into stars. "Some of them just can't believe that I'm serious," admits Shaffer. "Or that they're going to lose their job or have to change their behavior because of this crazy culture dimension. But the culture dimension will provide us with the adaptivity and flexibility we will need to take advantage of emerging markets and technology."

While changing the corporate culture and empowering people may not be urgent in the short term, when a company is struggling for its survival and trying to reverse financial losses, Shaffer warns, problems will arise should long-term needs continue to go unnoticed. "That's how railroads go into decline, how whole industries develop ill-adaptive thought processes. If we're going to try to run this company to the year 2019 and beyond, we're going to clearly have some thought processes we don't have now."

Keeping Your Vision in Context

We've heard it said a hundred times: Most visions are formulated into mission statements of vapid verbiage, and like horoscopes, there is usually something in there to placate everyone. Sure, companies write nice words, but then it's back to business as usual. We not only agree but have a remedy: *Separate your vision from your mission statement, then focus on the vision.*

An organization is a dynamic entity that, much like an amoeba, changes form as it grows. The culture, or context, will mirror the leadership, employees, markets, products, geography, and competition. Each company's context is unique. That's why Nordstrom's policy of helping the customer, no matter what, may work only in that environment. It is part of the company's unique culture that, in turn, is reflected in their vision. Anywhere else, the effort would be contrived, making it difficult for other companies to say, "This is a good idea," and simply make it their own. Only by becoming converts who are willing to set about to change their company culture can they even hope to succeed.

For the same reasons, you cannot set about reinventing your company's vision without a clear understanding of the culture. This explains, in part, the monumental task former IBM CEO John Akers faced when he tried to change the company and reverse recent losses. He talked about change without reinventing the corporate culture. Current CEO Lou Gerstner, on the other hand, didn't come up the ladder at IBM. As an outsider, he had to understand the culture he was entering before he could begin to create a new culture—one tied to his vision. With enough employee buy-in, the vision, coupled with the talent in the company, may be enough to revitalize IBM.

> **You cannot set about reinventing your company's vision without a clear understanding of the culture.**

For these reasons, any effort to create a vision that reflects the company, and in turn will be reflected in the actions and attitudes of that company, must begin with a seven-step process. We call this the

What Are We?

Sometimes it helps to use a show-and-tell method to get people to articulate their thoughts about the company. We suggest making a game out of the process in order to remove the stigma of right or wrong answers and help your employees express what they are really feeling. Here are a few questions you can throw out to the staff: What kind of animal best describes our company? Elephant, dinosaur, gazelle? What kind of food best describes the business? Pick a historical leader who represents the CEO. Is it George Washington? Or Hitler? Or Susan B. Anthony? Can you think of a fairy tale that serves as an analogy for our company? Or have everyone vote for the animal that best represents the business?

If you have a particularly creative group, invite them to draw pictures or write poems that express the mood or culture of the company. Post the responses and invite a general discussion.

organizational audit. This is a companywide exercise because the answers to all the questions cannot come exclusively from the top.

Step 1: Identify the Current Culture

The organizational audit requires input from everyone—customers, employees, and suppliers. Here is a sampling of the kinds of questions you need to be asking: What assumptions are we making about our strategic position and customer needs that may no longer be valid? Which functional units are most influential, and will they be as important in the future as they were in the past? Should we be moving into other areas in anticipation of future change? What are the key systems that drive our customers' businesses? What are our core competencies and the skills of our enterprise? What are the shared values and idiosyncrasies that comprise the organizational being?

If explored in depth, these types of questions will generate responses that, taken together, paint a picture of how things really work. What this is, is the basis for a strategic exercise that will force you to move through the decision-making processes that go on internally and externally. You will have to understand not only how customers make purchase decisions but also how employees make business decisions.

Step 2: Evaluate the Current Culture

Once you understand your company's culture, you can decide if anything needs to change. What should you be doing differently? What current aspects of the culture need reinforcing?

In the process, you probably will wrestle with some difficult dilemmas facing the business, dilemmas that must eventually be reflected in the vision. For example: Can you or should you change your business to accommodate a customer's needs? The first thing you will have to determine, based on your organizational audit, is whether the customer's request is reasonable or something you want to incorporate into your vision. If upon close inspection, you decide it is an aberration, perhaps you have to revise the customer's expectations or replace that customer with another. If, however, you discover that most customers have the same complaints or demands, you will have to review your business processes to see what you can do to accommodate change. Perhaps you can outsource parts of the process in a piecework fashion. Just-in-time inventory is a concept much in the mainstream today. Does it have a useful application in your business? Maybe, maybe not. Most people, however, are willing to play by your rules, if you establish them up front. On the other hand, there will be times when you won't get the business because your process or way of doing business won't serve their needs.

Your vision should reflect what the company is willing to do for a customer. Then if you find yourself straying from your vision, you may need to evaluate the situation carefully; look to see if the issues can be resolved by discussing the problems with employees and the customer. If the issues do not go away, you probably should find a new customer.

Step 3: Integrate Your Vision into the Culture

Once you have a complete picture of your organization, you can set about integrating your new understanding into some sort of corporate vision. This step probably should start with senior management but then extend throughout the company. At Holt, Hughes & Stamell, we started by writing down our personal visions for the company. They ran the gamut from such basic economic statements as "to exceed the rate of inflation by 15 percent" and "to make money," to more visionary responses, such as "to participate in a global economic renaissance." We then posted the responses on the markerboard where we could examine them and isolate the common elements. We found common verbs and adjectives and phrases, which we used to write a vision statement that reflected our common objectives.

Step 4: Get Everyone's Input

Run the results of management's exercise up the corporate flagpole, not to see who salutes but to serve as a starting point for a companywide discussion. With our version of the vision as an icebreaker, we took our whole staff through the same process. We wrote their objectives for the company on the markerboard, compared them with our vision, found the common ground, and together created a new statement. At this point, a company is about as close to universal buy-in as it is ever going to get. Now comes the hard part—living up to the words.

Step 5: Reflect Vision in Performance Objectives

This vision statement is the equivalent of a contract not only between the company and its customers but between the company and its employees as well. Management, therefore, must tie in individual performance objectives and measurements. For example, if your vision is to deliver the finest quality in its price class, then the goals for your sales force might be as follows:

1. Identify six new distributors for our products in the next quarter. Ensure that each prospect is compatible with our goals of providing excellence and good value.
2. Strengthen relationships with existing distributors. Set an example by providing distributors with the level of customer service we expect them to provide to their customers. *Help* distributors determine how they can sell our products more effectively and, in the process, in greater quantity.
3. Observe not only their rapport with customers but also their efforts to position our products to the buying public.

If you find this is difficult to do, then something is wrong with your vision statement. Either your organizational audit was not thorough or your vision does not reflect the true culture. It's back to the drawing board for you.

Step 6: Walk and Talk the Vision

At this point, all employees should feel enfranchised and be willing to lay down body and soul for the beliefs they took an active hand in forming. They have, in effect, become co-leaders themselves because they are committed to, rather than merely complying with, a vision they helped to shape. Now everyone, and especially management, must walk the walk, and talk the talk.

The vision must mean the same thing, whether the employee is securely ensconced in a corner office in corporate headquarters or standing on the loading dock. Leadership plays an important role in turning a concept into reality both through the type of environment it creates and by its willingness to live by the words. As senior managers, you serve as the role models for the rest of the company. If employees don't see management buy-in, they will assume that the whole exercise is nothing more than the "Program of the Month" and return to business as usual.

> **If employees don't see management buy-in, they will assume that the whole exercise is nothing more than the "Program of the Month" and return to business as usual.**

Step 7: Repeat the First Six Steps at Regular Intervals

As you add more people, the common ground is going to shift. This is especially true when companies grow through mergers and acquisitions. It's the difference between IBM and an entrepreneurial company like Lotus. Similarly, a conglomerate of corporate cultures—even warring cultures—can dilute or confuse the vision. This is a common plague among agencies that merge to expand their expertise, and it has led to the breakup of more than one company, with Saatchi and Saatchi perhaps the best-known example. You can't meld cultures; you need to start fresh.

If a company is growing quickly and adding new employees regularly, you may find you need to repeat the steps as often as every six months. Our rule of thumb is that whenever you are at a point where you are not interacting with every employee in some way, you are at risk of having low buy-in. If you repeat the process often enough, you do not necessarily have to institutionalize a formal process. Rather, to keep the company on track, you may only have to raise issues at staff meetings and

Establish a Cultural Benchmark

You've completed an organizational audit and reinvented your vision, and employee buy-in is at its height. Now is the time to establish a benchmark. Here's a little self-test to perform: What time do people come in? What time do they leave? What is the norm? What do customers notice first about the company? What do suppliers notice first?

To get the answers, you need to do a little research: Walk the floors and talk with a few customers and suppliers. Record your findings and save them. This is your benchmark, your early-warning signal when conditions begin to change. Every few weeks you should repeat the process. When the responses appear noticeably different from your benchmark, it's time for action.

tailor your actions. *We suggest creating a set of five questions you feel serve as a barometer for the company.* Answer these questions weekly. If you are not comfortable with the answers, it's time for a reevaluation.

Ever since we at Holt, Hughes & Stamell acknowledged ourselves to be struggling with the Pollyanna syndrome, we have been looking for ways to put and keep our business on the right course. Much of that effort has been directed internally in an effort to understand our culture and, if necessary, change it and create a vision for the business with broad employee buy-in. We felt we could not recommend this path to you, our readers, without evaluating the results. Therefore, we have interviewed several of our own employees to determine whether our efforts are paying off. We believe that their comments not only suggest that the methods we are proposing do work but also reinforce our belief that everyone wins in an environment of honesty and open communication. And if you ever thought your employees didn't know or care about what was going on, these remarks should serve to change your mind on that score:

- Even just in the year I've been here, we've gone through incredible change. We're all taller. In not having a formal structure, I was able to find the weaknesses in myself and build on these.
- We talk about institutionalizing risk, and all this other stuff. There are days when you do come in and think this is a bunch of hooey. But most of the time it's what we do. It's really enriching,

exciting, scary. It's a don't-take-anything-for-face-value attitude. Look beyond that and go further with it.

- People used to be given assignments on a kind of defined territorial boundary within their function. That's changed.
- It's a two-way street, when the company changes me and the changes in me change the company in an ongoing, back-and-forth process.
- When things started coming a little unstuck in the office, I was in a position where I could capitalize on opportunities, things I saw with my unique mind, my unique eyes, and sort of take the initiative without having to wait to see how it's going to be perceived by somebody else.
- This kind of change could be disconcerting to some people. There's a lot of deep exploring. But in a way, it's part of the challenge to come in every day and you still don't know where the thing is going.
- The Pollyanna memo began to clarify where I wanted to go, where I wasn't before, and I was glad for the exercise.

Integration in Practice

When Gerhard Heiberg tackled the task of pulling together the 1994 Winter Olympics in Lillehammer, Norway, he faced numerous challenges on all fronts—organizational, social, cultural, and environmental. We include his story here because in his words you will find virtually all the messages we have expressed in this book. You can see how he pulled a nation together by institutionalizing risk, establishing communication, creating a vision, providing leadership, and, above all, integrating all the elements into a strategy he shared with the participants.

Heiberg needed to overcome three major obstacles for Norway to be successful: (1) Neither the government nor the people understood the dimensions of what they had undertaken, (2) the people were not of one mind about the Olympics and were therefore unprepared to cooperate, and (3) a lot of people lacked motivation to tackle the job. The following interview excerpts explain how success was achieved.

Authors: How did you set about the task?

Heiberg: It's very important to get the people involved, and to do that you have to have everyone communicating among themselves.

To get that communication going, you need to build confidence among the people. They have to understand that communication is a two-way system . . . I had to get people involved in the thinking and the understanding of what we were about to do. [They needed to understand] that the dimensions were much greater than they thought and that they would have to face the music and be part of the process, part of the decision making.

Authors: Once you get people involved, how do you keep them moving forward?

Heiberg: You have to motivate people. I saw immediately that to get things going I needed the enthusiasm, the motivation of the people. How? First of all, you have to be motivated yourself. You have to know that this is the right thing, this is what we want, this is interesting, this is a lot of fun. We will create a success together. Second, you have to get them involved. You have to ask their opinions. You have to show that you are interested in what they are saying. You have to take them seriously . . . Little by little they are motivated, and then you get them understanding what you are trying to do. Thus the motivation leads to the fact that they understand what's happening and are willing to take responsibility for the project . . . Everybody has to take part in it or the project will not work . . .

I had to get the whole country moving. Because it was a question of convincing the parliament, the government, the whole country, about the importance of what we had taken on . . . The board of directors . . . became almost like missionaries in different parts of the country to get everything going, and little by little arose the enthusiasm, which was necessary. This has a lot to do with psychology and understanding how people are motivated.

One method Heiberg used most effectively was to pose tasks as questions. Rather than telling people do this or do that, he asked them how a task should be accomplished—after all, they were the ones who would have to do it or oversee it. Such was the case in developing the venues without destroying the ambiance of the cities and towns. "Ask questions of the people themselves," he explained. "Otherwise they'll be going to the papers saying that they are furious, this is not what they had in mind and they had always been against it. When I found people shouting like that, it was a question of getting them involved."

Although a Norwegian, Heiberg was viewed as something of an outsider—a successful businessman who had worked for several international companies and lived outside the Lillehammer area. To gain people's trust, he needed to change their perception. At the same time, he feels, his position as an "outsider" may have enabled him to see the big picture and find a way to deal with all the localized problems: "I went there and sat down with them. I met the mayor, the whole community, I met the people from broadcasting and from the press to try and explain that I'm not coming here as a king, I'm coming as one of you. I bring some specialties, you have other talents, so let's start communicating. Let's talk about this. So by being there, by dressing like them, talking like them, showing that I paid them respect and that I would work harder with them—that together we were going to make a success out of this. That's the way, little by little, I was accepted and felt they had confidence in me, that I would not let them down. [From that point on] it was much easier to get people to understand what this was about and feel not only part of it but responsible for making it a success."

Heiberg handled the environmental issues the same way. Environmental organizations both national and international were concerned that the Viking Ship speed skating arena was going to damage a bird sanctuary. To protect the land, they wanted to get rid of the Olympic Games. "I felt, if you can't beat them join them . . . I said, 'I can promise you that we will take environmental consideration into everything we do.' We started a process. The government became involved. The organizations were involved, and little by little, we got an understanding, we got confidence, and they were involved in all the planning. It was a question of changing the mentality of people in my own organization. They felt happy because they saw that they were taken seriously. We felt very happy because we felt this was part of the Norwegian image abroad that we take the environment into consideration."

Heiberg prefers to work within an organization, with people who have a stake in the project and its outcome. "You need to know the organization. You need to understand, not just tell them what and how we are going to do things. Get them involved and start the planning together . . . I can see

"You need to know the organization. You need to understand, not just tell them what and how we are going to do things. Get them involved and start the planning together . . ."

the easiest way is to get a so-called specialist in and have him organize everything, but still you need people to do the job. You don't want to fire everybody . . . You will have to change a lot of people on the way to change the whole mentality, but that's not the way you should start."

> *Authors:* After months of preparation, the event must have seemed almost anticlimactic. How did you keep everyone focused on the job during the Games?
>
> *Heiberg:* One week before the Olympic Games started, I called in all the people working in our organization, absolutely everybody, and asked, "If we should start all over, what would we have done differently?" I did that to make people feel secure and sure this was going to be a success and that we are on the right track because the answer was nothing. We would do the same things again, and that gave everybody the assurance that, yes, this is going to be a success . . . I think that our success was based on the fact that we managed to have enthusiasm and motivation in the whole Norwegian people and that's what came across to the United States and every other country in the world . . .
>
> We had to delegate the responsibilities to the various venues, to the villages, so that they could operate on their own knowing that it was completely up to them to make the decisions. But, of course, they were very well prepared for this. The planning had been very good. The communication functioned very well, and the flow of information was very important, so that at the time they had to make a decision out on a venue, they knew that they had all the information necessary, they didn't have to ask anybody.

Although it's important for CEOs to check their egos at the door, Heiberg says it is critical that they know themselves, know their strengths and weaknesses, and are willing to do something about it: "They need enough confidence in themselves to have a starting point or basis but at the same time that they are open and humble enough to accept that other people can do better jobs in different areas . . . By talking to others they can also develop as leaders and managers, and that is very, very important when you start growing."

Authors: In the end, what component is most critical to team building?

Heiberg: Communication must move in both directions—up and down the ladder. You accept the fact that they have thoughts and feelings about you and the way you operate, and they need to accept the same things . . . You have to be willing to reason; otherwise it will not function . . . Most people are afraid to speak up in the beginning so you have to convey the confidence that we are together in this and give them the feeling that your success is my success and my success is your success. You want to build a team . . . Small kingdoms do not work; people have to cooperate across the lines, across departments.

The Olympics was a massive project: 800 people working on a regular basis, 10,000 volunteers for the cultural program, and another 8,000 volunteers working for other sponsors. Part of the challenge was to keep the volunteers motivated for 16 days with no pay, sleeping quarters with 30 to a room, and the expectation that they would be available to help 24 hours a day. And when it was over, 90 percent of the paid employees were unemployed once again.

One of the reasons Norway took on the games was to increase employment and start the country looking into the future. It meant changing their outlook on the world and changing their ability to accept new challenges. Heiberg feels confident this has begun to happen. They are learning to move in the larger world without giving up their own cultural heritage. Norway is more open to foreigners. At the same time, the Games were done the Norwegian way, taking into consideration the culture, heritage and friendliness of the people.

We feel the lessons here of communication, integration, leadership, and vision are invaluable. The proof is in the post-Games success of most of the young people who worked in the organization. Although it took several months of looking and interviewing, the majority have found jobs with good companies.

You have one more stop before your final destination. Here are a few ideas to slip into your flight bag:

- To integrate all of a company's departments, divisions, and people, communicate across the artificial barriers of job description, authority, and responsibility.
- Remember, nothing in business occurs in a vacuum. Everything is interrelated and interdependent.
- Marketing is not a magic cure for a poorly conceived product.
- Create your vision in the context of the company's culture.

Give Power to Your People

"Never tell people how to do things. Tell them what to do, and they will surprise you with their ingenuity."
—General George S. Patton

Building a Bridge to Employees

While we already have identified a number of ways for employees to contribute to your company's ongoing success, the subject deserves more specific attention. In the final analysis, the success or failure of every company comes down to its people and how they function within the business, both collectively and as individuals. With all the investments management makes in its human resource departments, such as staff training programs and efforts to "empower" employees, it would seem that people should not be an issue. In fact, nothing could be further from the truth.

These days, in an effort to keep companies profitable, management often seems to put the extra burden on its employees. For example, when people are laid off or when positions are left unfilled after someone leaves or retires, the work seldom goes away. The other employees must pick up the slack. Increasingly today we hear our friends and fellow workers complaining about long hours, too much stress, not enough opportunity to move ahead, and too little control over their lives. We see many of these same people responding by becoming either compulsive workaholics or totally turned-off and unmotivated.

Another common belief in the 90s is that loyalty is a thing of the past. Management assumes that people will jump ship at any opportunity for better pay or higher position, while employees know that in today's world of mergers, acquisitions, and increased competition anyone is subject to being laid off. But even if we can't instill the kind of loyalty companies and employees used to share, we can improve the quality of the working relationship— the contract, if you will, between employee and company and vice versa.

Finding solutions requires striking a balance among the many perspectives, work styles, and attitudes that together make up a staff.

It doesn't matter if you have 3 employees, 30 employees, 300 employees, or 30,000, problems will arise. Finding solutions requires striking a balance among the many perspectives, work styles, and attitudes that together make up a staff. In our own company, for example, we have found one of the challenges is to create a work environment that satisfies the needs of two types of employees—the independents, who do their best work when given the freedom to act and think, and the main-streamers, who want to know exactly what is expected of them and, in some cases, be led.

Our struggle over whether or not to create an employee manual is a perfect example of the dilemma we face. A number of employees have told us they felt lost when they first came to our company. They didn't know the rules or understand the culture and would have liked something in writing. While an employee manual might be useful or comforting, we still think there is some value in allowing employees to figure it out and form their own judgments. A manual, after all, is only going to include the issues we feel comfortable discussing or can even recognize. There is a lot about our company's, or any company's, culture that insiders simply cannot see. We also happen to be of the mind that a manual destroys individuality and creativity. We'd rather that people experiment, knowing that others will tell them—without punishing or criticizing—when they are moving contrary to the culture or have crossed some invisible line.

If we have one rule of thumb that has come out of the months we have spent wrestling with the Pollyanna syndrome, it is our belief in the importance of seeing each person not only as an individual but as someone who contributes to the company in the larger context of the whole organization. This, of course, is the ideal. Progress, more typically, is marked in terms of individual achievement, which at its best is reflected in promotions and at its worst leads to the cutthroat political infighting that goes on in many companies. Augmenting individual success with a collective success requires re-creating the corporate culture and creating an environment that is—dare we say it—more spiritual. We use this word cautiously because it conjures up images of a touchy-feely, quasi-religious experience.

In fact, when we use the word *spirituality,* we are trying to redefine the role of work in people's lives. The problem is that most of us define our work life separately from the rest of our life. We tend to think: I go to work, I put in my hours, then I go home, and that's when I have fun—with my family, with a hobby, or through some other outside interest or organization that gives pleasure. Some of us connect with a church group, others with hiking or doing things with our children on weekends.

But given the number of hours we spend working, wouldn't it be better if we could find fulfillment and satisfaction at the office? In our efforts to help all of us—staff and management alike—find greater satisfaction, we have identified several effective ways to counter the effects of creeping Pollyannaism. The remedies fall into three general categories: (1) learning to work *with* employees rather than talk *at* them, (2) relinquishing some measure of control and allowing the business to seek its natural course, and (3) creating a vision statement that accurately describes the company culture.

Challenge Your People

One of our early efforts at Holt, Hughes & Stamell has been to make six management-level changes designed to benefit the experiences of everyone—management and staff.

1. A More Interactive Style

We have moved away from telling people what to do and started "asking" for help, ideas, advice, opinions, and solutions. In this way, we can create an environment that challenges people and encourages them to experiment and take risks beyond what they consider safe. Both the company and the individuals benefit from the creativity and new ideas generated.

As part of this effort, management no longer chairs every staff meeting. We rotate, and each employee will chair one or two meetings a year. The chair is responsible for coming up with a creative format for starting each meeting. At first, people relied on practical jokes, entertainment, and a lot of wisecracking, and we considered reverting back to the classic old approach of going down a punch list of issues. We took control again, but only so we could create a model for the meetings—to show by doing. We began giving structured presentations on a wide range of topics; others have not only emulated these talks but gone on beyond anything we imagined. Topics have included multimedia presentations on the Internet, discussions of classical music, a mock Egyptian mummification, and a creative dance lesson.

2. More Education and Training

Half of each staff meeting is now devoted to training and discussing topics of general interest to the firm, rather than specific accounts. In those cases where we feel employees would benefit from an outside program, we want to be certain they understand why they are taking the class and what they should accomplish. In most cases, management should have firsthand experience with the training program prior to sending employees. In all cases, training is not a substitute for dealing honestly and directly with an employee's weakness or shortcoming.

3. More Mentoring

Mentoring can take many forms. In the classic sense, it's a one-on-one relationship between an employee and a senior staff person. One of the problems with individual mentoring, we have found, is it's not a two-way street. Senior people tend to "tell" the person they are mentoring how they did it, when, in fact, time and circumstances may be radically different.

Rather, we are exploring methods of group mentoring, using our staff meetings as a vehicle for discussing and working together. Like most processes, it has its pluses and minuses. While some people thrive in this open forum for discussion, others find it a risky environment and hesitate to speak out for fear of looking stupid.

The best solution for us may be to use our staff meetings to praise examples of employees who exemplify our vision—examples of behavior, attitude, and work we feel fulfill what we are about. This way people can see the connection between actions and mission. Further, it reinforces for people how serious we are about our goals. For example, the concept of institutionalizing risk is not easy to explain. And even after we've explained it, employees still might not be convinced we really mean it—that we want them to speak out and share ideas, even challenge senior staff. But when we praise someone for taking a risk, we have not only given a clear example but also proved we walk the talk.

4. More Commitment to Research and Development

Besides providing obvious benefits to the business in having additional skills to offer our clients, employees who develop new talents are the real winners. They have the chance to expand their abilities and excel in areas that will be important sources of growth for the business. Rather than forcing people to compete for a limited number of top positions within the current business, R&D enables us to increase the opportunities and expand the company at the same time. Employees have taken the challenge in different ways: One person plans to use a sabbatical to explore opportunities to grow our international business. Others are working on ideas to expand our company into new areas of business.

5. Better Hiring Practices

How often have you told someone who interviewed for a job that he or she was "overqualified"? Well, believe it or not, this may be just the person you *should* hire. Obviously the better your talent pool, the farther and faster employees will move ahead. Provided you keep them happy and challenged, they are more likely to grow within your firm rather than leaving for larger, greener pastures. Increasingly we are trying to hire people who will fit with where we want to be rather than with where we are today. In some cases, this may require paying someone who is overqualified a bit more than the primary job is worth. On the other hand, you are probably getting more than you paid for in terms of skills and capacity for growth.

6. Closer Evaluation of Current Personnel

This last component may require the most delicate handling. As much as you may want to give employees the leeway to grow, measure the rope you give them. You don't want them to hang themselves accidentally by pushing them into positions they are not yet ready to handle. While you want to encourage their growth by rewarding their efforts, you can't create a system of promotion similar to grade inflation by moving them ahead solely on the basis of past performance. The Peter Principle works.

Rather, we are making efforts to thoroughly evaluate each employee's strengths and weaknesses as they relate to our company's mission and vision. In this way we can more logically craft work teams that not only provide a balance of abilities but are tailored to each client's specific needs. Each group represents an aggregate of qualities that compensate for and complement each other. And in keeping with our efforts to change the way we interact, the groups are self-directed; there are no superiors or subordinates.

From Control to Chaos and a Natural State of Business

Out of the work of social scientists is coming an understanding of the negative power of control and a need to encourage chaos in order to bring us to a more natural state of organization. Control is an issue that goes against what is natural. If you can stop trying to control, you can open up to receiving "abundance"—good ideas, new directions,

Six Tips for Effective Staff Meetings

Most busy people hate meetings because most meetings just seem to waste time. Over the years, we've heard about many techniques for improving the quality of staff meetings, and we've tried several more. We think the following six ideas are worthy of mention.

1. The only thing worse than a staff meeting is a Monday-morning staff meeting. Plan your meetings for any other day of the week, except Friday. This way people can come to the office on Monday, plan their week, and get started with their work. Psychologically they'll be in a better frame of mind when you do meet because they will have had a chance to get organized and make a dent in the week's work.

2. Don't subscribe to the one-minute-manager approach that calls for taking the chairs out of the room in order to keep meetings short. This gives everyone the wrong message—that management thinks it can, and should, control the meeting—and employees are left knowing they are being manipulated. We broke the control pattern when we put employees in charge of presentations. Now, we feel, our meetings more or less seek their natural organization and objectives.

3. Don't think you're going to cover everything the company does in a single staff meeting. These sessions should be a balance of news (good and bad), thoughtful conversation, new ideas, and project reports. You can give more variety to your meetings by using different presentation mediums and allotting different amounts of time to different topics. And when discussing project-specific subjects, stick to information of a more universal nature—such as lessons learned and status and scheduling issues that involve several people in the room.

4. If you dislike staff meetings as much as we used to, be careful you don't limit these sessions to only those times when there is big news—firings, hirings, wins, and losses. You will condition the whole staff to expect the worst every time you get together. Hold regular meetings and always start with some general topic that is interesting to the entire group. Then go into specifics and, by all means, encourage the group to participate in the discussion, ask questions, offer suggestions, and generally learn about different projects and other people's work. Whatever you do, don't just go down the job list. It's a waste of a valuable opportunity and many hours of collective staff time. If you focus on the big picture, people will enjoy coming together to discuss and share and think.

5. Use the meeting as a teaching and mentoring opportunity that doesn't just come from management. There is a lot of talent in organizations—

some you may not know exists. Encourage it. Use it. Having each employee take a turn at chairing a meeting will bring out some of this creativity. And encourage everyone as a group to mentor one another.

6. When making presentations, take the Sesame Street approach: Throw out something new every 30 seconds—otherwise minds tend to wander. And use the kindergarten show-and-tell method (which, for adults, equates to multimedia) to make presentations interesting. Use pictures, music, computers, text, whatever. Keep your message simple and clear. Bombard your audience's senses. Everything in our lives is accelerated to the point where the old rhythm and cadence is gone, so take the sound bite or image bite approach. You'll actually make the experience more pleasant for yourself as well.

prosperity—however you want to define it. When you release control and stop trying to cram everything into some predefined box, you free yourself to move outside the box. And often this is where you'll discover your best ideas.

Since there are definite applications for the chaos theory in business, we interviewed Linda Whiteside for this book. Currently she is president of Phoenix Discoveries Group, which offers consulting services to organizations in an effort to weave more holistic principles into the fabric of the workplace. She helps guide organizations through the transformation away from ego, fear, and control and toward a higher order of spirituality and consciousness. Lest you think this process is some sort of vague mysticism, you should know that Whiteside is a computer scientist by training.

She explains her own epiphany as follows: "My interest in Organization Transformation (OT) started when I read Margaret Wheatley's book, *Leadership and the New Science.* She married the ideas coming out of quantum physics and chaos theory with Organizational Development (OD) and introduced the idea of self-organizing systems to me. At the same time, I was working on letting go of control in my life. I could see that self-organization is a naturally occurring event when you let go of control. The next piece of the puzzle came when I moved to Gabriola Island in Vancouver. I met some workshop leaders who teach the concept called *follow your energy.* I believe that our energy is the organizing principle behind self-organizing systems."

Whiteside feels traditional, almost evolutionary, efforts to change our workplace—whether through quality circles, market-driven quality, work groups, or some other flavor-of-the-month program—do not work. She explains: "As an employee, I have been a participant in many OD initiatives presented by companies. After the event, we all went away feeling good, but nothing ever seemed to change when we returned to our workplace. The initiatives had no lasting impact. Work would get busy, pressure would build up again, and all would be forgotten.

"Just before my shift into OD, I took a job with a fledgling company. In addition to my other duties, I came with a desire to make a positive contribution in the creation of the operating principles of the company. The management group all spoke about teamwork, openness, employee input—all the popular ideas. Later, I realized that the management group were all strong controllers and not willing to implement the concepts they had agreed to. The company failed, I believe, because the management group was caught up in the ego aspects of image and control."

Authors: Could you explain the transformation from control to chaos?

Whiteside: Conventional OD initiatives were born inside the paradigm of control. They deal with managing and reengineering; vision and mission; goals, techniques, and rules. As our environment evolves, control will no longer rule. Our new environment is demanding a new type of interaction—one of creating the moment . . . Conventional interventions will take us to conventional places. We cannot use control to escape from the paradigm of control. Control behavior is fear based, coming from our ego-selves. Transformation is all about letting go of control and allowing the natural state of self-organization to occur. So dealing with control is fundamentally a spiritual issue. It's about letting in the love and letting go of fear, about living in spirit rather than out of ego.

Authors: We sense you feel that the need for businesses to transform is more critical to their survival than to maintaining their competitive edge.

Whiteside: Yes. Out of our need for security, we have resorted to control and fear to meet our needs. But fear is the source of our own misfortunes! When we operate out of fear and negativity, we build walls that defend us against others. But the walls that keep us separate from what we fear also keep us separate from what we desire. If we dismantle the walls, we reclaim access to the bounty of the universe.

Authors: How does OT relate to employees?

Whiteside: Organizations have a resonance, which is born out of the founding members. When an organization is hiring, the principle of "like attracts like" comes into effect. Some candidates seem to fit better into the company than others. Their resonance matches that of the company. [It's not unlike the compatibility we seek in a mate or in friendships.] When choosing among candidates, I believe it is important to honor the resonance first. Selecting someone with a mismatching resonance will invite an abrasive relationship that is not good for the organization or the employee. The process of transformation will change the organizational resonance, at which point it is possible that the employees will no longer "fit" with the new resonance.

Once we accept the dangers of control, we are ready to begin the transformation process. We start by breaking the pattern of control. First, we need to acknowledge its presence in our different actions, much the way an alcoholic or drug abuser must admit to his or her addiction before the healing process can begin. We need to be honest in our assessments of our behavior. "Ego always lies," says Whiteside, "so if you choose honesty, you know you are not acting out of ego. A commitment to honesty breaks through the denial that ego uses to defend the status quo."

> **"A commitment to honesty breaks through the denial that ego uses to defend the status quo."**

Second, and closely related to the first, management needs to look long and hard at its company to identify the many forms control takes in that environment. "Transformation is born out of the decision to make a new choice in each moment," explains Whiteside. "The changes that need to happen are internal ones, not external."

Third, having recognized the controls, someone needs to break the pattern. "Change cannot happen until one member of the system chooses to become aware and conscious of their behaviors and refuses to play," she says. "It takes a great deal of stamina and commitment to be the first one to stop playing the game. When one member in the system (family or organization) stops playing the game, the other members usually resist the change at first, wanting to hold the illusion in place. But there is no positive benefit to being unconscious."

Sensitivity Training for Executives

If trading control for chaos and a natural state of organization is a big step for you, Linda Whiteside recommends that you create some exercises to stimulate your sensory systems so you will feel and hear more of what is going on around you—both in and outside the office. Imagine stepping outside of your body not only to observe your actions but also to focus more completely on everything going on around you. For a whole day, try not to just go through the paces but rather focus on each event. Watch yourself peeling an orange. Be more aware, as you ride a bicycle, row a boat, or even walk, of all the complex mechanics of balance and muscle control we take for granted. Once you are more comfortable with this process, try it at work. Observe the nuances of work relationships. Try to identify examples of ego and control as they occur.

Finally, in order to withstand the efforts to resist change we must be in touch with our spirituality. Whiteside talks a lot about spirituality in business, but not in a religious sense. She equates spirituality with the power to be in touch with one's inner self. Some of us might call this confidence or having the strength of our convictions. Whiteside focuses on the source of that power—spirituality. She explains the power of spirituality within a business environment: "For organizations, I think it is an issue of power and control. Spiritual people are not easily manipulated, and do not respond to fear tactics. Because control tactics will no longer work, organizations that encourage transformation of their employees must also transform."

As we began to consider all that Linda Whiteside said, we realized her natural organization went a long way to explaining the innate dislike we have had for formal business plans. We asked her how giving free rein to chaos and its resulting natural order meshed with the conventional need to plan for a business's growth. Her answer is, It doesn't. "Planning is a process that extrapolates the past and present into the future," she says. "As change accelerates, the past and present will no longer define the future. In chaos, the future will take on a life of its own. Plans will have less and less value, becoming obsolete before they can be implemented." She uses personal computers and software development as examples of growth businesses that are not linear and therefore cannot be planned.

Break Your Personal Control Patterns

Linda Whiteside suggests breaking our personal patterns as a starting point for individual transformation. Stop some of the things we do by force of habit, she says, whether they be staying up late or eating exactly at 7 PM or drinking three cups of coffee each day: "When you are living on the outside of the pattern, you can see clearly how automatic your behavior has become. After the exercise, you may choose to adopt the behavior again, but this time you can do it with awareness."

"We, as a species, will need to find a new way to create our dreams," she concludes. "I believe that consciously living in the moment is the way. The power of consciousness brings the power of choice. The choices we make in each moment will lead us to the future we desire if we follow our intuition and our energy."

To reach this ideal natural order, both organizations and individuals need to transform. As individuals, she believes, we can find a pleasure and happiness in our work that will take us farther than fear and need of a paycheck. To accomplish this, and in keeping with her notion of spirituality, she says we need to open ourselves to the full range of emotions—intense happiness and intense sorrow. "Intense emotions can be scary," Whiteside says, "so people often block their feelings . . . The first step in opening up to a greater intensity of feeling is to acknowledge the desire . . . The next step is to allow the feelings when they come, and not shut them down with the usual defense postures."

We realize that such complete transformation can be difficult and frightening. Where to start? How to proceed? What if it doesn't work? We suggest you might find more success if you ease into the process by applying transformational principles and altering your behavior to problems as you identify them. For example, when someone makes a mistake, such as giving a bad presentation before a client, instead of yelling and reprimanding, begin by thinking about the issue. Talk to others to see if your opinion is shared. Then when you address the person, you can be critical but also constructive—and less controlling. You don't have to tear a person apart to make a point. No one responds well to a screaming match or to a situation where he or she is forced to defend actions on the spot. Nor are people generally able to process the information and make a commitment to change. Tell the person who made the mistake to listen and think about what you've said. The pressure is off, rules are set, and each side listens before responding. Then a day or two later, let the employee speak while you listen. After both sides have spoken calmly, you are ready to discuss. You'll find this environment encourages people to be less defensive and more honest. As a result, both sides benefit.

Apply Your Company Vision Internally

Every company has a cultural context. For example, some businesses describe their style as aggressive: "We play hardball with the competition." Others are known for their internal politics: "If you want to move up the corporate ladder here, put on your track shoes with spikes and climb the backs of your fellow employees." Others try to impose a gentler approach, both externally and internally. And still other companies are known as pressure cookers: "We work 25 hours a day, and like it."

Because each style or context will naturally attract the type of employee who can thrive in that environment, it is important—both to the business and to the employees—to honestly present what you're about. This doesn't mean you want every employee to be a carbon copy of everyone else. Diversity is healthy; you need different strengths. But at least every prospective employee should have a clear view of what he or she is getting into. Besides, you don't want to sacrifice your vision to a minority interest just because someone doesn't understand what you are about.

Remember too that as a business grows, it adds more people. Over time, fewer and fewer people will have had the full historical experience that brought your company from its humble beginnings to the present. They don't know your roots. They don't remember when it was a one- or two-person shop run out of the garage or basement.

The military has its own way of dealing with this situation. It's called basic training, and everyone goes through it, which establishes some important common ground. No one can possibly go through boot camp and say he doesn't understand how the military works. He may discover it's not for him, but he certainly will understand the ground rules. Actually a lot of companies used to work this way. In the days before young people started coming out of school with BAs and MAs and MBAs, almost everyone started in the proverbial mailroom. Procter & Gamble's approach has been to start everyone working in the field, selling and meeting customers. The William Morris Agency in California imposes a formal training program. You'll see people in the William Morris mailroom, who know they are moving up, affecting the dress of the talent agents by wearing designer clothes and Armani suits.

At Holt, Hughes & Stamell we have taken a different approach. For one thing, we need specialists—designers, copy writers, account executives, public relations specialists—and with about 35 people we are not large enough to start everyone out at the bottom. Besides, we don't have a mailroom. Our approach, therefore, has been to develop a vision and statement of our mission that reflects what we are internally as well as externally. Most people are content to let their mission statement serve as a tactic or process—which by definition is controlling. We believe, however, that our statement is the clearest representation of who and what we are. As such, we take advantage of that visibility and use it to its fullest advantage.

As we've mentioned before, our mission is created by the group and needs to be revisited and revised as we grow, add employees, and change objectives. By stating our vision up front, we make it easier for employees to align their personal goals and vision with the company's goals and vision. And having taken an active role, employees are more likely to be committed than merely compliant. We have shared goals. Some people, for example, want and need a structured environment. They want to do their job and get a paycheck. The structure is part of their spiritual needs. Others hate this. So it's critical that our mission statement and vision accurately and honestly reflect the company.

Once you write a mission statement, implement it until it is time to change. This means making it part of your hiring practices and incorporating it into the formal review process. If you can't make a connection between the action and the mission, why are you doing it?

In the case of hiring, perhaps you should ask people to declare their personal vision up front. While you certainly want the benefits of diversity in your company and don't want carbon-copy employees, by asking a prospective employee for his or her vision you open the door for discussion. Both you and the job candidate can decide if it's a good match. Then if and when the vision changes, people who don't like the changes will move on without any recriminations. But if your vision or mission keeps vacillating, people get confused and disillusioned. They blame themselves, try to conform, and don't understand when it doesn't work out. Remember, firing a person should be viewed as almost more of a failure on management's part than the employee's.

What Country Do We Work In?

As you'll recall, in the box on page 166, we explored some methods for discovering just "what we are." Consider another international approach: When you go to a foreign country, you see things that help you draw conclusions about life in that country, such as the way people talk to each other. Are they loud and excitable or cool and reserved? Are they direct or indirect?

Now consider your company as a foreign country. It will help you identify your business culture, which can be difficult to express. Who are the Fordians or the Xeroxians? Who are the HHSians? Ask yourself: What kind of people are we? What language do we speak? Are we warm and excitable or cold and dispassionate? Quiet? Depressed? Which country do we resemble, Italy or Norway? Do we like the country we resemble?

Once you have who you think you are, try to identify the image your clients and prospective clients see. In our case, for example, our offices are nice. Fun images and art decorate our walls and, of course, we have the basketball court. In some ways this is a facade because there is a hardworking company behind the fun. The basketball court represents teamwork to us, not playtime. It is important that casual visitors to our office think they are visiting the "country" we think we represent.

Your Efforts Are Repaid

Our own experiences have shown us the value of being honest and candid with each other and with ourselves. As the saying goes, honesty begets honesty. Our efforts to give employees an honest picture of our company and to share with each individual our impressions of his or her work, presentations, attitudes, and anything else that comes up have been repaid in full. Our employees have greater loyalty and commitment toward the company and are beginning to show their comfort with our efforts to counter the Pollyanna syndrome by speaking out more freely about issues. Positive results are the most gratifying reward.

Similarly, Hannaford Bros. CEO Hugh Farrington feels "seeing the people develop and the company succeed in tandem" is the best part of the job. He explains: "People developing for the sake of people developing isn't what business is all about, but it's a great way to conduct business. So as the company has grown, a whole lot of people have stepped into new jobs, new responsibilities and grown with the company. The growth of one forces the growth of the other."

Authors: What do you do when employees don't measure up?

Farrington: You should make the assessment whether or not the person can get up to speed. I have always been an investor in people, and if somebody can get up to speed, I'm willing to invest my time and energy to do that. If they can't, cut your losses.

Authors: When you do see potential, what kind of investment do you make to bring a person along?

Farrington: I've probably done as much teaching in my business career as I ever would have in the classroom. A big chunk of it is communication, and another chunk is education. If people are going to perform well, then they have to know what they're doing.

Authors: Can you give an example of the process you're going through?

Farrington: I put a strong focus on being value leader [in our market] by reducing our costs and being able to charge lower prices. The corporate culture, as a result, is quite participative, and different parts of the organization have different degrees of power to do their jobs. We're still struggling a little bit with how to do that. We've got four experiments going, plus a lot of our cultural change is in communication. For example, if you looked at our accounting area, you'd see they are structured as a large group, which is even reflected in how they have organized their desks. They created their own vision of what they wanted to do and how they wanted to do it, within the framework of the company's vision. Bottom line: They can better do their jobs. That's happened virtually throughout this building in smaller groups and departments.

If you think that all this is nothing but some 90s experiment in raising the consciousness quotient in business, think again. Farrington and every other businessperson we spoke with have equated their methods to bottom-line results. And our own efforts have all been undertaken with the success of our business in mind. As Farrington explains, "I think we have, on a macro basis, taken the approach to grind our business and have succeeded. We've done it through a whole range of things—by being very competitive, by having programs like the consumer-accounts program we introduced 10 years ago or so, when we focused a lot of energy on the customers at the store level . . . We've been active managers and an active company in terms of where we want to go . . . But if we were going to drive toward being different from other people in our business, we had to consolidate. We had to take costs out of the business, and we became more efficient . . . The challenge is to keep this business vibrant and growing. Because business comes from somebody else—the pie is only so big—we really needed to have a growing, dynamic business in a challenging environment . . . Not everybody selling our product is going to be here five years from now. So we've got to position ourselves to be one of the prospering, surviving companies. That's not always easy or fun . . . It's constraining in the sense that it's very difficult to find the right people to fit into the world that you want to create."

In the case of Hannaford Bros., Farrington reports that their approach returns about 2.7 percent of sales to the bottom line after taxes in an industry (retail) in which the average is something less than 1 percent.

Top investment consultant Michael Stolper likewise combines business issues with people management. He too recognizes that important balance: "I love what I do. I have a good time every day and love the interaction with people, and it's highly compensated, which is terrific . . . The way we spend money on our people is to keep the body count low, hire the best people we can find, and make sure nobody ever leaves for money . . . I try to hire people who test better than I do at every opportunity. It is more important that I have administrative skills."

Perhaps no one we spoke with has worked harder in the last few years to change a company's corporate culture and employee attitudes than Guy Gannett Communications CEO Jim Shaffer. He describes the fears and doubts he has faced as he has gone forward with his efforts to awaken the staff and prepare them for the future of media: "We went public with our program to change our culture on May 1. I woke up on the morning of May 2 feeling like the Romans must have felt when they crossed the Rubicon. There was no going back. I had just gone public with a program of sweeping change, and probably 30 percent of our managers were going to turn over one way or another or encounter a change in career path as a result . . .

"We are trying to develop a culture that emphasizes skill acquisition, learning new organizational techniques, and adaptivity. The people we're developing now are probably going to be the people who contribute to the management of the company in the future as well as, I hope, the management of the company of the present. But the point is, this is not just being driven by some feel-good philosophy. This is being driven by the needs of the shareholders for capital preservation on a long-term basis . . . In fact, I have some big forceps and a surgical saw in my hand, and I'm saying relax, this won't hurt."

Sports media entrepreneur Rory Strunk puts a lot of stock in being able to recognize the critical balance between employee issues and business. As he explains: "You recognize it with frustration. You see that a certain side of people is unhappy; there's more edginess to people. We're in a situation where we still have a small staff, so if something gets out of whack, it's been easy to say, 'OK, wait a second, what's going on?' We have weekly staff meetings, and internal communication is really strong. When you're a two- or three-person business, you test things out with meetings.

"But as you get a little bit bigger critical things happen, and you can spend considerable time in meetings. But if you have good communication . . . you're going to be agile and you're going to have a dynamic workforce. You've got to recognize if things are falling through the cracks and why they're falling through the cracks. And why there might be this edginess to the staff. You get everyone together and you say, 'Hey, what's going on here? What are the problems?' You lay it out, you try to get the people to be as honest as they can. When you get down to the root of the problem, you say, 'OK, this is solvable' or 'This is not solvable.'

"We recently dealt with that this spring. We were growing at a very rapid pace and making big jumps into things, and we weren't putting a lot of time into crossing the t's and dotting the i's because we felt we had to move quickly. Then we retrenched a little bit. We said, 'OK, we have jumped a little past the gun, retrench a little bit, look at our situation and establish a clear set of priorities.' "

The Holistic Workplace

It used to be that our parents and grandparents stayed with one job for most of their lives, in large part to qualify for a pension. The switch to personal retirement programs, such as 401(k) plans, has shifted more of the responsibility onto the individual. It also has freed us to move about and pursue a career that reflects how we think and feel at different times in our lives.

Experts say we can expect to change careers every 10 years. If our drives and interests change or become refocused, we can seek out work that meets our new needs. And both technology and the global nature of business have created such a dynamic matrix to the economy now that it almost creates a new opportunity. We should look at these changes not as a negative. They are opportunities. Job hopping has become a part of our economy as employees move from company to company, position to position, or decide to go off on their own, and maybe even return to a business 10 years later.

It is quite common to go back to school or get some sort of special training to stay current with technology or to recreate oneself. It's the story of the woman who was laid off from a major discount retail chain. Rather than try to find a job with another retailer, she went back to school to become a paralegal. She plans to work in a legal aid capacity. It's also the assembly-line worker who trains to become an electronics technician, or the liberal arts student who goes back to school for an MBA and a corporate career.

> **It is quite common to go back to school or get some sort of special training to stay current with technology or to recreate oneself.**

Statistics suggest that if you remain healthy throughout your 50s you probably will live to well into your 80s or 90s. With all this time ahead of you, it's critical that you fill it with rewarding work.

Too many of us still try to retrofit our jobs into our lives because we think of work in terms of needing a job. Perhaps employees and companies need to adopt a new contract that better reflects our times. Maybe commitment today is best defined as "I promise to work here, and as long as I'm here I will do the best possible work, as long as you think that is important. If I detect that it's not important, then that's as far as my commitment goes."

The sooner we learn to connect with the spirituality of what we do for 8, 10, or 12 hours a day, the better. For this is the only way to be fulfilled. Don't let your employees discover the relationship they should have had only when it's too late.

Congratulations, you have reached your destination. But it's not the end of your journey. This is a round-trip excursion. So pack a few more items in your flight bag and prepare to take off again:

- Challenge your people by keeping them involved in all phases of the business. Communication, mentoring, and good meetings are a few of the techniques you can use.

- Stop trying to control every aspect of the business. Relax and let chaos lead you to a more natural state of organization.

- Make your mission statement and vision reflect your company's internal and external goals.

Epilogue: Become a Frequent Traveler

"The whole object of travel is not to set foot on foreign land; it is at last to set foot on one's own country as a foreign land."
Gilbert K. Chesterton

Congratulations, you are on your way. Like a baby who has learned to walk, you have taken your most difficult steps. We know; after all, we're all still toddlers ourselves.

"The longest part of the journey is said to be the passing of the gate," wrote prolific Roman writer Marcus Terentius Varro. *Celebrate Your Mistakes* has served as your first map to the far corners of Pollyanna's kingdom. But if you have found a renewed sense of direction within these pages, learned how to celebrate your mistakes, and even begun to put a few of our ideas to work in your business, you truly have passed through the gate. That's the good news.

Now for a dose of reality. Your journey—far from being over—is just beginning. Like the trip the ancient Chinese philosopher Lao-tzu described, your journey will take you a thousand miles, figuratively, and then some. What makes it easy, he noted so long ago, is that it begins simply—with one step.

Having taken that first step, your journey should never end. For as long as you remain in business, you must fend off the insidious early signs of the Pollyanna Syndrome. The only way you can fight back will be to chart a never-ending course of corporate discovery, using the exercises mapped out in this book as well as any you are inspired to create. You must practice watching your competition, listening to your customers, talking with employees, and learning from your mistakes—to name a few tasks—until the processes are second nature to you. Then, when you are convinced such behavior is becoming a way of business life for you and others in your company, be even more cautious. For it is almost certain that complacency lurks close by. Don't be surprised if you fail to recognize the first signs. Each new, potential infection of corporate complacency will likely be different.

If you have room to cram one more important lesson in your flight bag, consider this: Your final destination is not uncovering and curing the many symptoms of the Pollyanna syndrome that may plague you and your company. This is the journey of a lifetime. Consider your course to be the Mobius Strip of Corporate Self Discovery—ever coursing on in one great, wondrous, continuous loop.

You owe it to yourself to celebrate your first steps. Just enjoy in moderation. Think of this point as the day you arrive home from one leg of a long trip. You have only enough time to visit with the family, wash our clothes, and repack before you are off again. That is about all the hiatus you have time for before you begin again.

If you stay the course, your journey will take you through wonderful places where you will encounter enriching experiences. And because you will never travel the same road twice, you will forever witness new sights. As you become an experienced traveler, you will not doubt begin to forge your own trails. The only regret you are likely to have is that all this travel can't be captured by a frequent flyer mileage program.

Bon Voyage and safe journey. Perhaps our paths will cross.

Index

Pollyanna syndrome—*Cont.*
London black-cab drivers example, 7-8
market changeability and, 4-6, 8, 17
Polaroid example, 6-7
remedies for, 180
Strunk interview, 25
symptoms of, 6, 9
tips for avoiding, 21-22
warning signs in, 28
portfolio managers
learning from failure, 88-89
personality traits of, 53
price cutting, 32-34
The Prince (Machiavelli), 35
proactivating change, 35-37, 106

Rapid Ray's example, of niche marketing, 44
research and development, 162, 181
Resort Sports Network web site, 25
risk, institutionalizing, 91-96
breaking isolation barriers by, 60-61, 63
steps in, 94-96
valuing diverse views and, 91-94
Roth, R.
on competition, 72
on creativity, 130
on hiring consultants, 66-67
Ruettgers, M., 44

S. S. Kresge example, of Pollyanna syndrome, 20
salmon industry example, of isolation from market, 61, 123
Schultz, H., 42
Sculley, J., 38-40
self-organizing systems, 184-185
sensitivity exercises, 187
service marketing
customer attrition study and, 78-79
niche for, 41-44
Shaffer, J. B.
on assessing employee performance, 163-164
on changing company culture, 193-194
on employee needs, 164-165
on future of media, 115-117
on integrating organizations, 163
on managing turnarounds, 34-35
on new idea acceptance rates, 117

Shaffer, J. B.—*Cont.*
on sharing plans with employees, 100
on using outside consultants, 65-66
on valuing diversity, 92-93
Shakers example, of failure, 47
shipbuilding industry example, of failure, 47
Smith, M.
on competition, 73
on creative process, 139-140
on Internet, 143-144
on outside board of directors, 67-68
on sources of inspiration, 135
Smith, R. B., 45
Snapple Beverage Corporation example, of selling out, 118
solutions, focusing on, 108-109, 121-123
spheres of influence, in niche marketing, 37, 41
spirituality, 179, 184-185, 187
staff meetings, 183-184
standards for niche marketing success, 42
Stolper, M.
on Aster, 51
on contingency plans, 98-99
on employee management, 193
on Hubris Curve, 29
on ideal portfolio managers, 53
on resistance to change, 14-15
on studying customers, 78-79
on virtues of young people, 132
on vision statements, 100
Strunk, R.
on balancing employee issues with business, 194
on business plans, visions, and employees, 101-102, 145
on competition, 72-73
on creativity, 131
on customers, 77
on evolution of his business, 140-143
on Internet, 144-145
on most important issues in business, 25
on sources of inspiration, 134-135
success, 13-17, 84-90
analyzing as failure, 106
characteristics of, 35
criteria for measuring, 42-43
dangers of, 6, 13-17, 28-29
failure turning into, 84-91
Hubris Curve and, 29
requirements for, 51-54, 57

Thank you for choosing Irwin Professional Publishing for your information needs. If you are part of a corporation, professional association, or government agency, consider our newest option: Custom Publishing. This service helps you create customized books, manuals, and other materials from your organization's resources, selected chapters of our books, or both.

Irwin Professional Publishing books are also excellent resources for training/educational programs, premiums, and incentives. For information on volume discounts or custom publishing, call 1-800-634-3966.

Other books of interest to you from Irwin Professional Publishing . . .

THIS INDECISION IS FINAL

32 Management Secrets of Albert Einstein, Billie Holiday, and a Bunch of Other People Who Never Worked 9 to 5

Barry Gibbons

By fabricating a series of unlikely relationships with everyone from the British Prime Minister to the Dalai Lama, Barry Gibbons delivers hard-hitting, yet provocative advice on everything from derivatives to dissent. The outspoken Englishman—a 25-year veteran of the battle trenches of big business—is credited with the revival of Burger King, and was proclaimed by *Fortune* magazine as one of their "Turnaround Champs" in 1991.
ISBN:0–7863–0838–9

NOT JUST FOR CEOS

Sure-Fire Success Secrets for The Leader in Each of Us

John H. Zenger

In an easy-to-read, straightforward style, author Jack Zenger offers an unparalleled guide to succeeding in business today. Uncovering the key behaviors of top performers, he describes precisely what makes them effective and outlines how readers can follow in their path and shine. Zenger explains how everyone can provide leadership in their own arena of work.
ISBN: 0–7863–0528–2

THE PARADOX PRINCIPLES

How High-Performance Companies Manage Chaos, Complexity, and Contradiction to Achieve Superior Results

The Price Waterhouse Change Integration® Team

Based on the collective experience of The Price Waterhouse Change Integration® Team and ground breaking interviews with leading executives across the globe, *The Paradox Principles* shows how to balance the tensions and conflicts that challenge the progress and effectiveness of today's organizations.

Readers learn how to achieve unparalleled success by managing the chaos, complexity, and contradiction inherent in five central paradoxes.
ISBN:0–7863–0499–5

THE LEADER'S EDGE
Mastering the 5 Skills of Breakthrough Thinking
Guy Hale

Learning how to think, especially in these rapidly changing times, will unlock the doors that talent, motivation, and experience alone can't. *The Leader's Edge* provides the tools to master the "art" of thinking as well as the confidence to handle any business decision. Providing practical skills rather than philosophy alone, *The Leader's Edge* instructs readers on the five skills needed to think more accurately:

- Situation review
- Cause analysis
- Decision making
- Plan analysis
- Innovation

ISBN: 0–7863–0426–X